Kore-eda Hirokazu

Kore-eda Hirokazu

Contemporary Film Directors
Edited by Justus Nieland and Jennifer Fay

The Contemporary Film Directors series provides concise, well-written introductions to directors from around the world and from every level of the film industry. Its chief aims are to broaden our awareness of important artists, to give serious critical attention to their work, and to illustrate the variety and vitality of contemporary cinema. Contributors to the series include an array of internationally respected critics and academics. Each volume contains an incisive critical commentary, an informative interview with the director, and a detailed filmography.

A list of books in the series appears at the end of this book.

Kore-eda Hirokazu |

Marc Yamada

UNIVERSITY
OF
ILLINOIS
PRESS
URBANA,
CHICAGO,
AND
SPRINGFIELD

Frontispiece: Kore-eda Hirokazu at the Cannes Film Festival
by Georges Biard CC BY-SA 3.0

Names: Yamada, Marc, author.
Title: Kore-eda Hirokazu / Marc Yamada.
Description: Urbana : University of Illinois Press, [2023] | Series: Contemporary
  film directors | Includes bibliographical references and index.
Identifiers: LCCN 2022047674 (print) | LCCN 2022047675 (ebook) | ISBN
  9780252045127 (cloth) | ISBN 9780252087264 (paperback) | ISBN
  9780252054495 (ebook)
Subjects: LCSH: Koreeda, Hirokazu, 1962– —Criticism and interpretation.
  | Motion pictures—Japan—History. | BISCAC: PERFORMING ARTS / Film /
  Direction & Production | BIOGRAPHY & AUTOBIOGRAPHY / Entertainment &
  Performing Arts
Classification: LCC PN 1998.3.K674 Y36 2023 (print) | LCC PN 1998.3.K674 (ebook)
  | DDC 791.4302/33092—dc23/eng/20230124
LC record available at https://lccn.loc.gov/2022047674
LC ebook record available at https://lccn.loc.gov/2022047675

Contents

I owe a debt of gratitude to several individuals who aided in the completion of this book. First and foremost, thanks go to Kore-eda Hirokazu and his assistant, Fukuma Miyuki, who patiently responded to several inquiries and requests. Because Covid travel restrictions prevented an in-person meeting, Kore-eda and his team worked with me to locate interviews to include in this study that accurately represented the arc of his career. Appreciation is due to the best research assistant with whom I have ever had the pleasure to work—David "Dewey" Walter. It is hard to express how helpful it was to have an assistant knowledgeable in film with whom to brainstorm early in the process of researching and writing this manuscript. I would also like to acknowledge the support of BYU's Humanities Center and the College of Humanities for granting me the funds and the time away from teaching necessary to complete this project. The editors of the Contemporary Film Director series at the University of Illinois Press—Jennifer Fay, Justus Nieland, and Daniel Nasset—as well as the anonymous external reviewer, provided helpful guidance during the revision process. Finally, I give my deepest thanks to those who choose to share their space with me—M, K, and S.

Note: East Asian names appear in their native standard, with surname first.

Kore-eda Hirokazu |

Beyond Ozu and Loach: Kore-eda Hirokazu in Japanese and World Cinema

This book provides an intervention in the English-language criticism on one of the most acclaimed international auteurs working today, Kore-eda Hirokazu (b. 1962). During his thirty-year career, Kore-eda has directed over fifteen feature films, as well as numerous television documentaries and programs, many of which are commercially available around the world. As of 2022, Kore-eda's works available on disk, through streaming services, and online include *Lessons from a Calf—Record at the Spring Class at Ina Elementary School* (*Mō hitotsu no kyōiku—Ina shōgakkō haru gumi no kiroku*, 1991); *August without Him* (*Kare no inai hachigatsu ga*, 1994); *Maborosi* (*Maboroshi no hikari*, 1995); *Without Memory* (*Kioku ga ushinawareta toki*, 1996); *After Life* (*Wandāfuru raifu*, 1998); *Distance* (*Disutansu*, 2001); *Nobody Knows* (*Dare mo shiranai*, 2004); *Hana: The Tale of the Reluctant Samurai* (*Hana yori mo naho*, 2006);

Still Walking (*Aruitemo aruitemo*, 2008); *Air Doll* (*Kūki ningyō*, 2009); *I Wish* (*Kiseki*, 2011); *Like Father, Like Son* (*Soshite chichi ni naru*, 2013); *Our Little Sister* (*Umimachi diary*, 2015); *After the Storm* (*Umi yori no mada fukaku*, 2016); *The Third Murder* (*Sandome no satsujin*, 2017); *Shoplifters* (*Manbiki kazoku*, 2018); *La vérité / The Truth / Shinjitsu* (2019); and *Broker* (*Beurokeo*, 2022). Since launching his career in the early 1990s as a documentarian, Kore-eda has won dozens of awards for his films at festivals around the world, particularly at the Cannes Film Festival, where he took home the Jury Prize for *Like Father, Like Son* in 2013 and the Palme d'Or for *Shoplifters* in 2018.

While a steady stream of criticism on Kore-eda's work has appeared in Japanese, English, and other languages over the past few decades, much of this scholarship reinforces the identification of his films as manifestations of the values of traditional Japanese cinema.[1] The extensive use of static camerawork and austere shot compositions in his first feature film, *Maborosi*, prompted inevitable comparisons to traditional Japanese aesthetics. Japanese and non-Japanese critics alike ascribed the values of minimalism and a sensitivity to ephemerality to *Maborosi*, reinforcing timeworn ways of viewing Japanese culture through traditional perspectives.[2] Japanese filmmaker Higuchi Naofumi, for instance, recognizes in *Maborosi* and other Kore-eda films an exemplification of the aesthetic value of *mono no aware*, or a sensitivity to the transient nature of things ("Narushishizumu"). For his part, Kore-eda claims not to have consciously based the cinematic style of *Maborosi* on the aesthetics of traditional forms such as Zen Buddhism: "When I went to European film festivals with *Maborosi*, people often spoke about Zen. They asked me about the relationship between the film and Zen. That was something I never thought about" (Schilling and Kore-eda 15). Considering these early characterizations of his work, critics often place the director in a lineage of filmmakers from the golden age of Japanese cinema in the 1950s and 1960s such as Ozu Yasujirō (1903–63), the famed director of *Tokyo Story* (*Tokyo monogatari*, 1953) and other classics of Japanese cinema whose meditative works were also associated with traditional aesthetics and religious perspectives by film critics such as Paul Schrader, who likens Ozu's films to Zen concepts.[3] Critic Yoshimoto Mitsuhiro comments on the essentializing tendencies of American critical approaches to Japanese film: "Very schematically, the history of American scholarship on Japanese cinema can be divided into three phases: (1) humanistic celebration of great auteurs and Japanese culture in the 1960s, (2) formalistic and Marxist celebration of Japanese cinema as an alternative to the classical Hollywood cinema in the 1970s, and (3) critical reexamination of the preceding approaches through the introduction of discourse of Otherness and cross-cultural analysis in the 1980s" (8).

Although we cannot separate Kore-eda's work from the national lineage of which he is a part or redetermine how that lineage has been characterized in criticism, foregrounding the "Japaneseness" of his films misses an opportunity to consider the way his work is shaped by issues and conditions that extend across cultural boundaries and impact other capitalist traditions around the world. International audiences do not seek out Kore-eda's films for their depictions of an exotic Japan, as they have in the past with directors such as Kurosawa Akira (1910–98); instead, audiences appreciate the films' humanistic portrayal of families and individuals struggling to connect and survive in modern times. For this reason, the goal of this book is to introduce a fresh critical framework for viewing Kore-eda's films within an international context, one that seeks to reinterpret the characteristics attached to his cinematic works by viewing them in relation to the contemporary socioeconomic concerns with which filmmakers outside Japan also engage in their work. This is not to say that Kore-eda deliberately conceals or obscures aspects of Japanese society and culture in his films; indeed, most of his films are set in recognizable areas in Japan and feature ethnically Japanese people speaking Japanese. Yet his films also do not perform Japanese culture to essentialize it as distinctive and exotic.

Focusing attention away from traditional aesthetics, this book argues that *excess*, not minimalism, is the central feature of Kore-eda's brand of humanism. I use the term *excess* in accordance with its original meaning in film studies, as a key concept in the 1970s to describe the shift away from a critical focus on the unifying narrative of film texts toward a consideration of the opposing and heterogeneous forces that escape and exceed these narrative systems and organizational systems outside the cinematic text (Thompson 130). Conforming to this view of cinematic excess, Kore-eda's films, I argue, manifest moments when a desire for human connection escapes the logic of the systems and policies formed in the implementation of neoliberal values, a process that has shaped social conditions and cultural expression—even filmmaking—in Japan over the last thirty years. These moments of excess are captured through images of bodies that form shared spaces as they move, perform, and assemble on both sides of the camera, bodies that manifest the humanistic impulse of Kore-eda's films, which serves as the basis of his appeal around the world.

Kore-eda's unconventional path to becoming an international filmmaker provides him critical distance from a national tradition that he both looks to for inspiration and seeks to overcome. Born in 1962 amid Japan's meteoric rise to the status of a First World country after its defeat during World War II, Kore-eda was raised for the first few years of his life in the northern Tokyo city of Nerima, part of the larger metropolitan area of the Japanese capital. At the age of nine, he moved with his family to the Asahigaoka area of the neighboring city of Kiyose, settling into one of the *danchi* (large public housing complexes) built between the 1950s and 1970s to accommodate the families of "salarymen," or company workers who fueled Japan's growth during this period. He lived in the complex throughout his college years, eventually moving out at age twenty-eight. Kore-eda's recollections of his family life in the Kiyose complex reveal the challenges and dysfunctions that characterize many of the everyday families he features in his films and documentaries. The absentee father figures that appear in several Kore-eda films reflect the director's ambivalence toward his own father, a veteran of World War II and a humble factory worker (Kore-eda, "Chichi no shakkin" 384). Born as a Japanese national in Taiwan, a colony under Japanese rule from 1895 to 1945, Kore-eda's father fought for his country in China during the war. After the Soviet invasion of Manchuria in 1945, he was sent to a Siberian prison camp, where he endured three years of hard labor, abuse, and other horrors before making his way back to his defeated country. Though Kore-eda's father rarely spoke about his experience in the war, PTSD impacted his reintegration into society and domestic life. He would often disappear from home for long stretches at a time, racking up gambling debts that burdened his wife and children with financial struggles (386). Kore-eda recalls creditors harassing the family during his father's regular benders while his mother frantically scraped together enough cash to pay them off, relying on government welfare to make ends meet (387). Kore-eda's financial struggles as a youth manifest themselves through his attention to issues of poverty and social benefits in the films *Nobody Knows*, *After the Storm*, and *Shoplifters* and in his television documentary *However . . . in the Time of Government Aid Cuts* (*Shikashi . . . fukushi kirisute no jidai ni*, 1991).

Due to the lack of a consistent paternal presence in his home, Kore-eda was raised by his mother, grandmother, and two older sisters—an aspect of his youth, Kore-eda suggests, that gives his films a female perspective, including his most autobiographical offering, *After the Storm* (Kanazawa and Kore-eda 52). The film focuses on the middle-class Shinoda family, consisting of a matriarch, Yoshiko, and her two grown children, Chinatsu, a mother of two, and Ryōta, a flash-in-the-pan novelist and degenerate gambler. Yoshiko's late husband, like Kore-eda's father, squandered his family's income on gambling before he died, frustrating Yoshiko's dream of moving out of her cramped apartment and into a proper house. To depict the restrictions of Yoshiko's meagre lifestyle, Kore-eda accentuated the cramped conditions of her apartment, setting the film in the same Nerima complex of his youth (Ogawa and Kore-eda 60–62). Inspired by Kore-eda's memories of growing up, profligate men are often treated as sympathetic characters in films such as *After the Storm* and *Our Little Sister*, taken care of by women who have a soft spot for the men's struggles.

Kore-eda's path to becoming a director was shaped more by happenstance than by a focused drive to make films early on. After high school he attended Waseda University, a member of the elite Big6 league of Tokyo universities, which equates roughly to the Ivy League in the United States. Renowned for its literary traditions, Waseda is the alma mater of several famous Japanese writers, including international bestselling author Murakami Haruki (b. 1950). With ambitions to become a novelist, Kore-eda entered the Faculty of Letters in the School of Arts and Sciences but was quickly drawn to the world of film and scriptwriting (Yamada and Kore-eda 263). Like other Japanese universities at the time, Waseda lacked a proper film program that could direct Kore-eda's early training in the cinematic arts. Aspiring filmmakers from Kore-eda's generation gravitated instead to college cinema clubs that produced Super 8 films or studied with luminaries such as film critic Hasumi Shigehiko, who guided the careers of many young directors from the 1990s, including Kurosawa Kiyoshi (b. 1955) and Aoyama Shinji (b. 1964), among others (Nolletti, "Introduction" 2). Instead of seeking out filmmaking clubs, Kore-eda spent his time at Waseda reading screenplays and skipping class to watch Japanese and international classics at art house theaters in Tokyo (Ogawa and Kore-eda 57). Sitting through three hundred to four hundred films a year, Kore-eda focused on the great auteurs; he was particularly drawn to the films of Federico Fellini (1920–93) and described the moment he discovered the films of the Italian great as a "turning point" in his growth toward becoming a director (Risker 42). Kore-eda's sympathetic advisor allowed Kore-eda to write a screenplay, the first of many, instead of a thesis on literature, a requirement for graduation in his department (Ogawa and Kore-eda 57).

After graduating from Waseda in 1987, Kore-eda sought work as a scriptwriter—a profession in the film industry that he felt better suited his introverted nature than that of a director required to command a film set (Hokazono and Kore-eda 107). Realizing that it could take years to earn a stable living penning scripts, Kore-eda sought out every opportunity he could find to establish himself as a screenwriter, deciding on a whim to sit for an employment exam for television production, an industry that was more active in hiring than film at the time (Hokazono and Kore-eda 107). He landed a job with TV Man Union, the first independent television production company in Japan, as an assistant director of documentary programming. Before starting work with TV Man, Kore-eda had not had much interest in documentaries beyond the work of Ogawa Shinsuke (1935–92) and Tsuchimoto Noriaki (1928–2008), the two most well-known documentarists in Japan, and after only a year at TV Man, he was already languishing in his new trade. Unable to stomach the realities of an industry that required him to churn out content at breakneck speed, Kore-eda struggled to produce work in an expeditious fashion, becoming the target of ridicule by coworkers who grew impatient with his subpar work (107).

Fearing he was losing focus on the types of stories he wanted to capture on film, Kore-eda began secretly producing his own documentary, *Lessons from a Calf*, while continuing his day job at TV Man (Hokazono and Kore-eda 107). Inspired by a story he had read a few years earlier about children who raised a calf as a class project during the school year at a progressive elementary school in Ina City, in the Nagano prefecture, Kore-eda sought permission from the teacher to film the students as they prepared to raise another calf. Equipped with an 8mm camera he borrowed from work, he spent three years, from October 1988 to March 1991, commuting back and forth between rural Nagano and Tokyo to shoot footage of the class whenever he could sneak away from his duties at TV Man (107–08). During the forty-four-minute program, the mostly handheld camera captures the children preparing months ahead for the arrival of the calf, Laura, on loan from a local farm, by raising funds to pay for her feed and building her a stable. During the nine months Laura lives at the school, the children take turns caring for her needs, tearfully saying good-bye when she returns to the farm as a fully grown adult. Making a film in the welcoming countryside of the Nagano prefecture was just what Kore-eda needed after the rejection he experienced in the cutthroat Tokyo television industry (107). His work on *Lessons from a Calf* revealed Kore-eda's talents for capturing the world from a child's perspective—an ability that would earn him accolades by critics who identify him as one of the best directors of juvenile actors (Rafferty). Airing on Fuji Television's late-night documentary series, *Nonfix*, *Lessons from a Calf* impressed TV Man bosses, who promoted Kore-eda to the position of director, allowing him more freedom in choosing his projects. Two documentaries about activists followed. *However . . . in the Time of Government Aid Cuts*, which also aired on *Nonfix*, examines the suicide of the former division chief of the Social Welfare Bureau of the Ministry of Health, Labour and Welfare, Yamanouchi Toyonori, who grew frustrated by the bureau's refusal to authorize welfare assistance for those in need—a topic with which Kore-eda could relate, having grown up on government support. The documentary portrays the suffering of welfare recipients and the diffident attitude of administrators toward social benefits in an age of cutbacks. After shooting *Lessons from a Calf* on an 8mm camera by himself, Kore-eda was provided a crew for *August without Him* and other productions, allowing him to focus on his work as director and interviewer during productions. In *August without Him*, Kore-eda depicts the final months of Hirata Yutaka, the first openly gay AIDS patient in Japan, a marginalized figure in Japanese society at a time when the social stigma of homosexuality and AIDS was still quite strong.

Based on this early work, it is possible to situate Kore-eda in the tradition of Japanese documentary filmmaking. His work on *Lessons from a Calf* and the emphasis he gives to individuals with disabilities place his works in conversation with some of the early works of filmmakers such as Tsuchimoto, Hani Susumu (b. 1928), Hara Kazuo (b. 1945), and Satō Makoto (1957–2008). Yet Kore-eda's innovation as a filmmaker is based in his blending of feature film and documentary stylistics. Accordingly, Kore-eda's early work in documentary filmmaking influences his feature films, though the balance between his dependence on these two mediums changes with each new project (Kore-eda, "Dokyumentari" 82). In his second feature film, *After Life*, Kore-eda mixes elements of documentary production and feature filmmaking to see what kinds of stories emerge from the process (Jia and Kore-eda 16).[4] *After Life* tells of a group of recently deceased individuals who spend a week at a way station between life and death before moving on. At the beginning of this seven-day period, the deceased are greeted by caseworkers, who inform them that during the week they must choose one memory from their life that they will take with them to eternity. The caseworkers adapt the memory into a short film and screen it for the visitors at the end of the week. In making the film, Kore-eda hired several college students to conduct interviews with people on the street, asking them to describe one memory that they would choose to take with them after they die, just like the interviewers in the movie ask the guests at the way station (Sōda 104). Kore-eda used the five hundred interviews that his staff collected on videotape to form the screenplay of *After Life*, incorporating ideas for memories from the interviews and even casting a select group of subjects to play themselves in the film (104). Kore-eda followed the same process years later while creating *The Truth*; he conducted extensive interviews with both Juliette Binoche and Catherine Deneuve, who star in the film, before beginning to shoot (Arai 18). Some of the questions that he asked Deneuve—"What actress imparted to you her DNA?" and "To whom have you imparted your DNA as an actress?"—made their way into the final cut as part of an interview between Deneuve's character, Fabienne, and a journalist that opens the film (18). Kore-eda shot 2004's *Nobody Knows*, moreover, like a documentary. The film is based on an actual event that occurred in 1988: "Nishi-sugamo kodomo okizari jiken" (the affair of the four abandoned children of Nishi-Sugamo), in which five children were found in squalid conditions in a Tokyo apartment, having been abandoned by their mother for six months (two of the children were deceased—a baby, whose body was discovered in the apartment, and another child, who was discovered buried in the mountains). To capture the immediacy of events, Kore-eda paused after shooting each scene to edit the footage instead of waiting until all the shooting was wrapped, following a pattern he uses when making his documentaries (Jonze and Kore-eda 49).

Kore-eda lacks formal training as a cinematographer, but his understanding of the technical side of film production has grown with each movie he has made. Early on, Kore-eda often utilized techniques of cinema verité and direct cinema associated with documentary filmmaking to lend an aura of authenticity to his fictions. He used handheld footage in *After Life* and *Distance* to capture movement without smooth tracking to create the energy and immediacy of the home movie experience, but he also favors an observational style that manifests through static wide shots in films such as *Maborosi*, using naturalistic editing and lighting and a spare sound design to relay a sense of authenticity. He claims that producing documentary programming sharpened his skills in capturing the nuances of human interactions in his feature films (Hokazono and Kore-eda 107–08). After *Nobody Knows*, however, Kore-eda's films have taken on more of a commercial feel. He still uses his trademark observational style of static wide shots mixed with handheld camera footage at times in his films, but he also incorporates effects such as sliding cameras and push-in shots to give his compositions a more dynamic feel in films such as *Air Doll* and includes more nondiegetic sound to accentuate emotional and dramatic moments in films such as *Our Little Sister*. In most of his feature films, Kore-eda favors shooting on 35mm lenses, though at times he uses telephoto focal lengths to capture characters in their larger environment. Preferring the texture and grain of film stock, Kore-eda has nevertheless acknowledged the rapid conversion to digital over the last ten years, opting to shoot his 2017 feature, *The Third Murder*, in digital anamorphic widescreen, though he argues that some of the poetry of film is lost due to this change (Chang).

After directing several documentaries in the early 1990s, Kore-eda leveraged the experiences and resources he garnered with his early success at TV Man to create his first feature film, *Maborosi*, which debuted at the Venice Film Festival in September 1995 and became the standard by which his feature film career would be evaluated. *Maborosi* would go on to receive critical accolades for its use of lighting and cinematography, earning Kore-eda some of his first awards as a filmmaker, including the Golden Osella for Best Cinematography at Venice and the Dragons and Tigers Award at the 1995 Vancouver International Film Festival. Reflecting Kore-eda's original interest in literary fiction, the film takes as its source material a novella he read as a college student, *Maboroshi no hikari* (1983), by Japanese writer Miyamoto Teru (b. 1947). Having just dealt with the subject of grief in *However . . . in the Time of Government Aid Cuts*, Kore-eda felt that adapting a novel about enduring the loss of loved ones, a central theme of *Maboroshi no hikari*, seemed like a fitting way to transition between documentary and feature filmmaking (Feinsod and Kore-eda).

Although both *However . . . in the Time of Government Aid Cuts* and *Maborosi* feature the struggles of a single mother dealing with the loss of the family's breadwinner, critics overlooked connections between *Maborosi* and the themes Kore-eda was developing in his socially conscious documentaries, seeking instead to locate the film within classical Japanese cinema by referencing Ozu's *Tokyo Story*. Following *Maborosi's* North American premiere at the Toronto International Film Festival in the fall of 1995, articles likening the film to Ozu's works by David Desser, Christine Marran, and Bert Cardullo, among other critics, appeared in film publications. Comparisons to Ozu in early scholarship and criticism would follow Kore-eda for the next twenty-five years, becoming a customary way for critics to situate his work within Japanese and world cinema. Even today, it is hard to find an article or review of his films that does not rely on references to Ozu as a way of contextualizing Kore-eda's career. Adam Bingham, for instance, argues that Kore-eda has "enshrined Ozu," as well as the themes of domesticity and the quotidian practices of daily routine that characterize his films (101). For his part, Kore-eda acknowledges a debt to Ozu in the development of his cinematic style, admitting that the pacing and the representation of time in his films are influenced by Ozu's family dramas (Rirī and Kore-eda, "Egakō" 210). Taking a page from Ozu's preshooting preparations, moreover, Kore-eda holds a yearly retreat for members of his production company, Bunbuku, to work on scripts and prepare for shoots at the same inn in the coastal area of Kanagawa where Ozu used to work on his own films (Arai 13).

The characterization of Ozu as a traditional filmmaker is complicated by the way that the cinematic great is representative of golden age cinema from the 1950s and 1960s, as well as an innovative alternative to the classical Hollywood style that was dominant during the 1950s. Prominent film scholars such as David Bordwell and Hasumi Shigehiko associate the inventive techniques that Ozu used in his films with a modernist style, but others identify Ozu as a standard-bearer of classical Japanese film. Their efforts to connect Kore-eda's work with Ozu are based in a nostalgia for the golden age, as well as an inability to place Kore-eda's films within the limited generic options available to classify contemporary independent cinema. The 1970s and 1980s saw the decline of a film industry that blossomed during the golden age. The loosening of restrictions imposed by US occupational forces, which sought to stamp out feudal values in the immediate aftermath of World War II, along with the increase in the wealth of the nation led to the development of a studio system in the 1950s that, like its American counterpart in Hollywood, was dominated by well-known companies such as Tōhō, Shōchiku, Nikkatsu, and Tōei. The most renowned filmmakers in Japanese history—including Ozu, Naruse Mikio (1905–69), Mizoguchi Kenji (1898–1956), and Kurosawa Akira, among others—produced some of the classics of Japanese cinema during this time. New Wave directors such as Oshima Nagisa (1932–2013) revitalized the industry in the 1960s through thematic and stylistic experimentations, but with the rise in the popularity of television in the 1970s, the Japanese film industry fell into decline. Close to bankruptcy in the 1970s and 1980s, studios began cranking out mostly animation for younger audiences, adaptations of popular television dramas for adults, and nostalgia for the older generation to keep up with popular demand. Although Japanese film experienced a resurgence in the 1990s driven by a new crop of independent filmmakers, classifying their work in what had become a largely market-driven industry grew more difficult, requiring filmmakers to find a place working in recognizable global brands. However, unlike the films of Kurosawa Kiyoshi—whose *Cure* (*Kyua*, 1997), *Pulse* (*Kairō*, 2001), and *Loft* (2005) embody the Japanese horror boom of the late 1990s and early 2000s—Kore-eda's work was much harder to place in

Japanese film, prompting critics to associate elements of the cinematic and television genre *shomingeki* (home drama) to his work.

For his part, Kore-eda is not completely comfortable in Ozu's shadow. Although he admits to imitating Ozu's style in *Maborosi*, a choice he now regrets, Kore-eda does not innocently replicate the style of his progenitor (Hase 124). Instead, much of Kore-eda's work can be viewed as commentary on Japanese cinematic history itself—commentary that offers him critical distance from the tradition. This critical distance is evident in his layered treatment of two iconic aspects of Ozu's work that have come to overrepresent Kore-eda's own style. Ozu's "tatami shots," taken from a camera positioned close to the floor, capture domestic scenes in films such as *Late Spring* (*Banshun*, 1949) and *Tokyo Story*. Likewise, Ozu's signature use of "pillow shots," transitional shots of seemingly random images of everyday life interspersed within the film, are used by Kore-eda in *Maborosi* in a clear reference to Ozu's work (Desser, "Imagination"). Yet if *Maborosi* seamlessly incorporates these techniques, *After Life* comments on the challenge of directors to manage the "anxiety of influence" through its use of them. In helping an elderly man named Watanabe Ichirō decide on a single moment from his humdrum life to transform into a film, the workers provide him footage of his entire life on a set of seventy-one VHS cassettes, one for each year he was alive, which Ichirō spends several hours during the week perusing. On one of these tapes, a tatami shot captures a middle-aged Ichirō seated on the floor eating breakfast while his wife works in the kitchen behind him. But the film-within-a-film structure makes it clear that we are not just watching the daily life of a couple but rather a metatreatment of Ozu's style, unlike the use of tatami shots in *Maborosi*. This additional level of subtext turns the scene from a transparent depiction of the past into a rumination on the way memory, like film, mediates our experiences. Avoiding some of the more dramatic moments in his life, Ichirō eventually chooses a simple memory of sitting on a park bench with his wife—a scene captured in a long shot that recalls contemplative moments in Ozu's work, particularly *Tokyo Story* (Desser, "*After Life*" 60). By referencing Ozu, Desser argues, the film self-consciously incorporates a common theme of Ozu's films—making the most of a mundane existence—into a story in which people learn to make peace with their mortal lives by watching films (60).

Figure 1. Kore-eda references Ozu in
this tatami shot from *After Life*.

An alternative way of situating Kore-eda in Japanese film rather than as a return to golden age cinema is through television. Kore-eda is part of a cadre of directors who were originally trained in the TV industry and lacked experience working within the studio system. Other TV-trained filmmakers include Hani, Ōbayashi Nobihiko (1938–2020), and Suwa Nobuhiro (b. 1960). Accordingly, Kore-eda's self-conscious treatment of the *shomingeki* genre acknowledges his place in the Japanese television and cinematic tradition while opening up creative space from it. In *Still Walking* and *After the Storm*, Kore-eda revitalizes the home drama and its realistic portrayal of the everyday lives of ordinary people by turning to the directors and writers known for their work in the genre. For *Still Walking*, a film about a family that comes together to commemorate the death of their eldest son, Kore-eda studied the work of two well-known figures associated with the home drama, director Naruse, recognized for his bleak depictions of the struggles of his female protagonists in films such as *When a Woman Ascends the Stairs* (*Onna ga kaidan wo agaru toki*, 1960), and screenwriter Mukōda Kuniko (1929–81), an award-winning essayist and short story writer who penned several screenplays for television programs during the 1960s and 1970s. Studying Mukōda's work, particularly *Like Asura* (*Ashura no gotoku*)—serialized on Japan's public broadcasting channel, NHK, from 1979 to 1980—Kore-eda learned how to craft dialogue for domestic settings, while Naruse's films helped him grasp the technical side of location scouting and the nuances of blocking scenes and staging exchanges between characters within the close quarters of a Japanese home (Kanazawa and Kore-eda 52). The influence of these two on *Still Walking* and *After the Storm* is evident in scenes in which characters hold private conversations in cramped kitchens, hallways, and the small corners of the houses and apartments that serve as the setting for these domestic dramas. Yet, as with his treatment of Ozu's work in *After Life*, Kore-eda does not innocently copy the home-drama formula. Rather, he self-consciously draws attention to the layers of meaning produced through the filming of family memories. In her reading of Kore-eda's use of the home-drama style in *Still Walking*, Mitsuyo Wada-Marciano argues that Kore-eda's generic mimicry activates the memory function of the audience through allusions to works of classical Japanese cinema with which they would be acquainted, such as Ozu's *Tokyo Story* and *Late Spring* ("Dialogue" 117). References to the hot summer weather, shots of characters staring out at the ocean, and cinematography that obfuscates point of view, among other things, recall Ozu's *Tokyo Story* and *Late Spring*, allowing Kore-eda to acknowledge his place in the Japanese cinematic tradition while using the themes that emerge from this layered treatment of film to extend the metacinematic depiction of memory and filmmaking to the process of reception (116).

The impulse to create distance from the cinematic lineage of the golden age in Kore-eda's work is also reflected in his attempts to remain independent from the major studios that produced the classics from this era. In a 2004 conversation with Kurosawa Kazuko, daughter of famed director Kurosawa Akira, Kore-eda expressed longing for the creative freedom he enjoyed while working independently of the major studios in his first four films (274). Although Kore-eda would go on to partner with Shōchiku for *Hana* and Tōhō for *Our Little Sister*, independent filmmaking in Japan and around the world—as he noted in a 2014 discussion with Chinese director Jia Zhangke (b. 1970)—has experienced a renaissance with the growth of foreign sources of financing that fund the projects of young filmmakers, giving them autonomy from major studios (Zhangke and Kore-eda 21). Freedom from the commercial demands of studio films has allowed Kore-eda's work to straddle the divide between art house and entertainment as he seeks a balance between the two. While he complains about the melodramatic mode of television, he often casts TV stars in his films, suggesting an impulse to move beyond the art house style that characterizes his early work and to make films with broader appeal (Rayns, "Acts" 137). Most of his films fall somewhere in the range between these two poles. According to critic Higuchi Naofumi, only two of Kore-eda's films can be considered pure art house—*Maborosi* and *Air Doll*—and only two can be considered pure entertainment—*Like Father, Like Son* and *Our Little Sister*—with most of his work like *After the Storm*, which is representative of his larger oeuvre, blending the two styles ("Kore-eda" 30).

Kore-eda's sensitivity to the popular interests of his audience is a product of his work on commercials and music videos. In addition to his documentaries and feature films, Kore-eda directed fifteen TV spots for Nissan, Sony, and other companies, along with several music videos for pop groups such as AKB48 and for the singer-songwriter Cocco, with whom he also collaborated on the feature-length documentary *So It's Alright: Cocco's Endless Journey* (*Daijōbu de aru yōni: Cocco owaranai tabi*, 2008), which covers the Okinawa-born singer's tour of 2007 and 2008. In 2021 Kore-eda signed a deal with Netflix for multiple projects, including a major feature film and a television series titled *The Makanai: Cooking for the Maiko House* (*Maiko-san chi no makanai-san*, 2023). The eight-episode series—for which Kore-eda serves as showrunner, codirector, and writer—is based on a popular manga series set in Kyoto at a house where apprentice geisha live together.

Kore-eda's familiarity with the world of global independent cinema allows him to engage the work of directors outside Japan whose films have influenced Kore-eda's development just as much as those from his national tradition. David Desser recognizes elements of post-1990s Asian art cinema in Kore-eda's use of "long takes and de-dramatized narratives" ("Imagination" 273). In particular, the use of minimal camera movement and improvised acting by Taiwanese New Wave director Hou Hsiao-hsien (b. 1947) in films such as *A City of Sadness* (*Bēiqíng chéngshì*, 1989) inspired Kore-eda's approach to capturing the experience of everyday individuals in his work.[5] Like Hou, Kore-eda quietly observes his characters and the spaces in which they reside without being overly concerned with developing plot. In a short piece that he wrote for a collection of essays in honor of Hou's work, Kore-eda reflected on things he learned from the Taiwanese auteur: "Films need people more than stories; Landscapes also harbor emotions. (Hou would often write on colored paper the characters that in Japanese read '天地有情,' which means 'Heaven and Earth Have Feelings.' These words caution against viewing the world in an anthropocentric way.) Life's details (for example, 'eating') should be respected; and 'music can blow like the wind through a scene'" ("Things"). In a strange bit of irony, Ozu's influence on Kore-eda's work may be a product of Ozu's influence on the films of Hou, a fan of Ozu who paid homage to Ozu's *Tokyo Story* in his 2003 film *Café Lumière* (*Kōhī jikō*), which played at a ceremony commemorating the golden age great. That Kore-eda received Ozu through Hou speaks to a more complicated process of transnational exchange in East Asian cinema than a linear model of succession within a national tradition suggests.

Moving beyond East Asia, Kore-eda's interest in the work of European directors such as the Belgian filmmaking duo the Dardenne brothers—Jean-Pierre (b. 1951) and Luc (b. 1954)—and British director Ken Loach (b. 1936) shaped the representation of socioeconomic issues in his films. The Dardennes' use of a handheld camera in *Rosetta* (1999) to track the struggles of an impoverished teenage girl to find employment influenced the style and thematic content of *Nobody Knows* and *Shoplifters*. Even more instrumental in the development of Kore-eda's attention to the socially marginalized in his films is the social realism of British director Ken Loach (Bradshaw). In an essay on the sixty-six films that have influenced him the most, Kore-eda identifies Loach—who, like Kore-eda, comes from a background in television—as his favorite director currently working ("Kore-eda Hirokazu" 25). In particular, he identifies Loach's *Kes* (1969), a story about a troubled boy who finds solace in raising a kestrel, as a formative influence on his work with child actors in films such as *Nobody Knows*, *I Wish*, and *Like Father, Like Son* (25). In preparation to shoot *Nobody Knows*, Kore-eda sought out Loach's advice on working with child actors, sharing a beer with the British filmmaker, who traveled to Japan in 2002 on a promotional tour for the film *Sweet Sixteen* (2002) (25).

Viewing Kore-eda's work in relation to Loach's socially conscious oeuvre reveals new meanings for the themes and visual motifs that Kore-eda develops in his narratives. Loach, who won the Palme d'Or for *I, Daniel Blake* in 2016, depicts the struggles of economic and social disadvantage in films such as *Riff-Raff* (1991) and *My Name Is Joe* (1998), showing how poverty and homelessness result from unequal economic arrangements that place burdens on social services. Yet in contrast to Loach's didacticism, Kore-eda brings subtlety to his treatment of socioeconomic concerns in his feature films, dealing overtly with poverty, for instance, in only a handful of works, such as *Nobody Knows* and *Shoplifters*.

Yet even if socioeconomic issues are not on the surface of Kore-eda's visual narratives, the subtext of the vast majority of his features and documentaries reflects the effects of the neoliberal policies that were incorporated in the 1980s in the United States, Great Britain, and Japan. Emphasizing the importance of free-market principles, neoliberalism has become the hegemonic form of capitalist globalization (Cooper 267). Although not a monolithic system in practice by any means, neoliberalism generally implies the privatization and commodification of public assets as well as a deregulation of market economies so that wealth is redistributed from a "downward" trajectory (by means of taxes, welfare, and entitlement programs) to an "upward" one through polices aimed to protect corporate entities (Elliot and Harkins 5). To enact privatization, neoliberal policies call for the "dismantling of public entitlements such as education, health, and welfare," placing more emphasis on individual responsibility (5). However, the impact of neoliberalism goes beyond just economic policies; it is an omnipresent force that has transformed conceptions of society and culture, shaping the way individuals identify themselves and the groups to which they belong. The emphasis placed on free-market values by policy makers, in particular, has impacted every facet of life, resulting in what Robert Marinov describes as the "economization of non-economic parts of life" (7). Under neoliberalism, argues Wendy Brown, the rationality of the market extends to every sphere of society and culture, even those spheres that are seemingly independent of its logic, emphasizing expediency and profit as central goals and transforming individuals into "entrepreneurial actors" in each segment of their daily lives (1).

At the same time, the implementation of neoliberal policies involves inherent contradictions, particularly the need for state intervention in order to create a free-market utopia. Neil Brenner and Nik Theodore recognize a "blatant disjuncture" between the ideals of neoliberalism and its practical application in society: "On the one hand, while neoliberalism aspires to create a 'utopia' of free markets liberated from all forms of state interference, it has in practice entailed a dramatic intensification of coercive, disciplinary forms of state intervention to impose market rule upon all aspects of social life" (5). This contradiction is at the heart of neoliberal practice in Japan, which emphasizes the role of government regulation in implementing political and economic policies (Lee 507). Spreading to Japan in the early 1980s under Prime Minister Nakasone Yasuhiro (1982–87), who was heavily influenced by the policies of US president Ronald Reagan and UK prime minister Margaret Thatcher, neoliberalism found new life in the 1990s and 2000s under the administrations of prime ministers Hashimoto Ryūtarō (1996–98) and Koizumi Jun'ichirō (2001–06) as part of the effort to pull Japan out of the recession of the 1990s and 2000s. In order to promote economic growth, Hashimoto sought to deregulate Japan's financial structure, welfare system, education, and health care. Using catch phrases such as "individual freedom of choice" and "personal responsibility" to promote self-reliance, the administration shifted the accountabilities of the government onto the citizenry by promoting austerity (Hayashi 180). Efforts to deregulate social institutions, then, reinforced systemic hierarchies by necessitating the creation of policies and practices to impose economic values onto citizens.

The state's off-loading of social responsibilities onto individuals and families created a society of winners and losers that negatively impacted social and familial cohesion. Deregulated labor markets during the 1980s and 1990s spurred growth but also increased the number of underpaid workers in dead-end jobs. These employment trends impacted the family structure, leading to a decline in marriage and birth rates and an increase in divorce. Youth bore the brunt of these social transformations. Those struggling in a diminished job market were branded by names that have come to represent the flip side of the optimistic image of the salaryman of the bubble economy in the 1980s (Gordon 80). Due to the decline of full-time employment opportunities in the private sector, *furītā* (a subclass of underemployed workers) grew in number during this time. Likewise, NEETs (individuals not in education, employment, or training) constituted a large segment of society—close to two million in 2002—that were neither employed in a full-time capacity nor seeking education or training to become part of the workforce in the future (80). The lack of economic opportunity led to the growth of the number of "parasite singles," young adults who live at home, hesitant to start their own families amid economic uncertainty.

Like Loach's work, Kore-eda's films depict the dehumanization that occurs because of the top-down foisting of neoliberal values onto Japanese society in the 1990s and 2000s and the appropriation of individuals and families as appendages of the larger economic interests of the state. At the same time, Kore-eda's films respond to the effects of a neoliberal worldview in a manner different from that of Loach, whose socialist politics as a long-standing supporter of the Labour Party in Britain are manifest in his explicit criticism of Britain's welfare system in films such as *I, Daniel Blake*. Part of the problem with the message of Loach's films, critics suggest, is that they present "an overt critique of capitalism whilst simultaneously operating within it" by partaking in the business of filmmaking (Archibald 25). Indeed, Loach's position as "the leader of a 'collective autocracy' on the film set" is part of a capitalist system that oppresses the working class and other disadvantaged groups while providing him greater possibilities in creating his visual narratives (35–37). Kore-eda, on the other hand, avoids polemical gestures in his films, opting for more oblique representations of political issues.[6] Even though the development of Kore-eda's film career in the 1990s parallels the growth of Japan's state-led neoliberalism, Kore-eda's films do not directly critique these policies, as he explained in an early interview: "I do not like films that have a social message, either fictional films or documentaries. It's all right if a film reflects something the maker has thought about and agonized about. But a message in film doesn't come from that sort of place. The filmmaker thinks he has the answer. But the world doesn't work that way" (Schilling and Kore-eda 13).

Kore-eda takes great efforts to resist the critical/complicit paradigm that is often used to characterize cultural texts vis-à-vis socioeconomic hegemony. His films sketch the effects of these neoliberal policies on social environments and on the individuals and groups that inhabit these spaces. Characters in his films do not stand outside these forces but are a product of them; the desire that gives form to their identity, familial connections, and social behavior is coded by the larger economic systems in which they reside. Yet just as the regulation of desire is inevitable in the organized systems of contemporary society, shaping identity and communal experience, so are the moments when desire spills over the very top-down control these systems impose. Kore-eda's films visualize this spillover of desire through nonorganized bodies and shared spaces that manifest as excesses of institutional logic. Utilizing the conceptual lens of *nonorganization*, the remaining sections in this book will examine the formation of shared spaces in filmmaking, family, urban landscapes, and memory to elucidate the basis of the humanistic focus of his films.

Nonorganized Labor and Shared Spaces of Collaboration in Kore-eda's Early Documentaries

Life would be suffocating if everything had a purpose.
—Kinami Kenji (Odagiri Jō) in *I Wish*

Unlike the bodies of resistance in Loach's films who battle the oppression of the socioeconomic systems that surround them—like the defiant blue-collar hero Daniel Blake—individual and collective bodies in Kore-eda's films do not stand apart from institutions such as the state, the corporation, and the family that regulate and direct the organization and movement of bodies under their purview but manifest as products of the very top-down control these institutions impose. Yet even within these systems of control, the forces of excess can escape systemic boundaries, as discussed in relation to cinematic excess above—a process at the basis of the humanistic focus of Kore-eda's films.

Describing the effect of excess in real-world systems, organizational behavior scholar Torkild Thanem uses the term *nonorganization*, which he develops primarily through a reading of the work of theorists Gilles Deleuze and Félix Guattari on embodiment and desire (203). I use Thanem's notion of nonorganization as a framework for viewing Kore-eda's films because it provides a way of representing the workings of the abstract forces of desire and excess within the real-world organizations that Kore-eda deals with in his films: families, corporations, communities, and film sets. In describing organizational dynamics, Thanem draws an important distinction between the notion of *disorganization*, which suggests anarchical forces that seek to dismantle ordered systems, and *nonorganization*, which describes the energies within these very ordered systems that can escape the hierarchies and structural boundaries imposed upon them (207). Nonorganizational forces emerge from within ordered systems, manifesting as an excess of their stratified organization in moments in which desire exceeds the function of the system (205). As Thanem states, nonorganization contributes "to the understanding of the messy forces that on the one hand are the implicit problems targeted by organizational activities and, on the other, disrupt, subvert and escape these activities" (204). As a product of both top-down systems of control and energies that escape these orders, nonorganized bodies never settle into a cohesive and unitary structure or organism, ever transforming through continual "processes of becoming" (212).

Imagining individuals, human collectives, and the spaces they occupy as nonorganized bodies allows Kore-eda to acknowledge the reality of the forces that shape social interaction while nevertheless giving expression to human desire. Indeed, this attention to human desire in Kore-eda's films provides the basis for the meaning of the label *humanistic*, which is often attributed to his work, a label that reflects the broad liberal values of democracy and human rights that characterize transnational trends in media, as well as the films screened at major international festivals such as Cannes and Sundance (Jenner 230–31). But at the same time, the wide-ranging principles of humanism do not perfectly encompass Kore-eda's worldview. Though bodies in Kore-eda's films are formed through desires for intimacy, communal bonding, and even a search for truth and meaning, they emerge not in resistance to established hierarchies in the larger order that surrounds characters and defines their individual and communal identities but rather as excesses of the very systematic operation of these orders. Kore-eda's sensitivity to the nuances and complexities of the human experience is couched within an effort to decenter an anthropocentric perspective and to acknowledge the larger forces that shape people's lives through a cinematic style that takes on posthumanistic qualities. As Kore-eda suggests, his use of a detached perspective in his features draws attention to the social realities that determine one's place in the world. Indeed, Kore-eda's characters rarely emerge victorious against the conditions that determine their fate as individuals and families, often succumbing to poverty, divorce, and other difficulties. They learn to find their place in the larger order of the world, to "choose the world over themselves," as the sixth-grade protagonist of *I Wish*, Ryūnōsuke, comes to understand when he fails to reunite his divorced parents. Yet excesses that result from the very act of repeatedly navigating these circumscribed worlds and performing assigned identities therein allow for moments of slippage from pre-scribed patterns of behavior—fathering children not of one's own blood, developing familial bonds around shoplifting, taking shortcuts through ordered city streets, and so forth—that expand and reimagine the bodies and territories created to demarcate human relationships.[7]

Before discussing the manifestation of nonorganization in Kore-eda's cinematic worlds, it is important to consider the way his films tell the story of how they are produced—how the very process of filmmaking for Kore-eda is built on the creative potential of both organization and nonorganization. My reading of Kore-eda's films extends beyond a her-meneutic attempt to uncover a stable source of meaning in his works as artifacts, considering instead the way Kore-eda's films are formed through the relationships between the physical bodies of filmmakers, subjects, and even the audience. A constructive relationship between the top-down control of the business of filmmaking and the unbound-edness of the creative process is reflected in Kore-eda's approach to shooting his movies, a process in which performances and relationships on set often exceed the parameters imposed by a hierarchical approach to film production. Certainly, one could argue that many films result from these dynamics, as film as a medium is fundamentally a collabora-tive project involving producers, directors, scriptwriters, set designers, cinematographers, editors, and other staff. Even actors play a role in the collaborative effects of creating films in the work of contemporary directors such as Korean auteur Hong Sang-soo (b. 1960), who rarely prepares scripts before shooting films such as *Right Now, Wrong Then* (*Jigeumeun-matgo-geuttaeneun-teullida*, 2015), relying instead on his actors' improvisational skills. Kore-eda's background in documentary filmmaking heightens the creative tension between these two forma-tive influences in his work. Like many directors, Kore-eda serves as the manager of a multimillion-dollar enterprise every time he creates a feature film, mobilizing a huge staff to help shape his vision into a product that will be bought and sold on the open market. The demands of independent filmmaking in Japan, in particular, require directors to play an even more central role in the process. Due to the dearth of skilled laborers trained in the various specialized skills required in film production, directors are often pressed to participate in all aspects of moviemaking—casting, writing, shooting, editing, and so forth (Paletz and Saito 53).[8] The executive demands placed on filmmakers account for Kore-eda's micromanaging tendencies and his reputation as a "control freak" on set (Rayns, "Review" 1). He wrote, directed, and edited most of his works since *After Life* while also serving as a producer on *Nobody Knows*, *Air Doll*, and *Shoplifters*. Particular about the staff and actors with whom he works, Kore-eda, like many directors, tends to collaborate with a group of the same personnel, who collectively belong to what has become known as the Kore-eda gumi, or the "Kore-eda Club" (Tsukada and Andō 24). Members of this club include cinematographer Yamazaki Yutaka and well-known actors such as Arata, Asano Tadanobu, Terajima Susumu, Natsukawa Yui, You, Fukuyama Masaharu, Maki Yōko, and Rirī Furankī, among others. Kore-eda was particularly fond of casting the late Kiki Kirin to play remembrances of his mother in *Still Walking* and *After the Storm* and Abe Hiroshi to play versions of himself in these two films (Kanazawa and Kore-eda 51).[9]

Kore-eda's hegemonic control over his early work is no more clearly reflected than in the production of his first feature, *Maborosi*, a film, Kore-eda suggests, on which he firmly left his stamp as a director (Michida and Kore-eda 118). Along with writing the script, which he completed before the start of shooting, Kore-eda sketched storyboards, designed the cinematography, collaborated on sound design, and even made the final decision on camera lenses (118). Reluctantly ceding the work of editing to renowned editor Ōshima Tomoyo, Kore-eda found it "frustrating" to not have complete control over even this one area of the film (Paletz and Saito 53). He even played a role in the promotion of *Maborosi* as it was distributed worldwide, handpicking a translator to compose English-language subtitles and bringing her along to interpret for him on foreign press junkets (Rayns, "Review" 1). The managerial control he exercised over the film is evident in the perfect symmetrical

Figure 2. Kore-eda regrets the overly
structured symmetry of shot compositions
like this one from *Maborosi*.

compositions that characterize the work—an artistic choice that, along with other aspects of the meticulous production, Kore-eda now regrets because they drained the final product of its vitality (Shimamori and Kore-eda 171).

Despite or perhaps due to this managerial control, moments in Kore-eda's documentaries and features abound when creative energy exceeds the boundaries formalized in film production. These moments are created through exchanges between filmmaker and subject that shape both. The potential for the shooting process to impact subjects and their experience is evident in Kore-eda's early works. Although he seeks to relay "an imperfect world" in all its complexity in his documentaries, the very presence of the camera can interfere with the ecosystem that he is attempting to capture and even with the reaction of his subjects, eliciting responses that they might not articulate under normal circumstances, which in turn shapes the story (Shimamori and Kore-eda 185). In his early work at TV Man, Kore-eda realized the need to restrain the "violent" potential of the camera and to approach subjects and their worlds with delicacy (180). An exchange with the teacher of the class featured in *Lessons from a Calf* helped him understand the need for filmmakers to honor their outsider status. The teacher thanked Kore-eda for his interest in the class project and assured him that his presence would benefit the students but also reminded Kore-eda that he was just a visitor at the school, without a place of his own (186).

Notwithstanding the caution he exercises in shooting subjects, however, Kore-eda often surpasses the limitations established by the standard procedures of documentary production. In contrast to the interview protocols practiced by public television, in which the physical presence and even the voice of the interviewer are removed from footage to maintain objectivity, the intimate relationship that Kore-eda develops with his subjects blurs the division separating interviewer and interviewee (Gerow and Kore-eda). Kore-eda's resistance to standard forms of objectivity provides an ethical function for the excess that escapes the hierarchical system of documentary production, aligning him with other practitioners of the genre of "participatory documentary" who seek to break down the artificial distance created between subject and filmmaker. Amid the blurring of lines between the two, the subject can have an effect on the filmmaker, Kore-eda believes, just as the filmmaker influences the subject's responses. This is because interviews do not pause daily life, Kore-eda suggests; they do not exist in a space outside the ongoing experience of both the subject and the filmmaker, whose objectivity is inevitably compromised in their interactions. At the same time, this loss of control as a filmmaker can be thrilling. There is no guidebook, Kore-eda suggests, on how to proceed when the association between interviewer and subject exceeds a formal relationship (Shimamori and Kore-eda 185). Kore-eda first became aware of the creative potential of this breakdown of boundaries when the children he was filming for a documentary about a school for the mentally disabled directly engaged his cameraman: "Until that point in my documentaries, I had separated the filming person and the filmed subject into two separate dimensions above and below a horizontal plane. But through making that documentary, I managed to build a vertical axis, and was able to film in a shared three-dimensional space. I thought at the time, 'this is what it means to represent the presence of the camera at the scene'" (Gerow and Kore-eda).

If the breakdown of roles disrupts objectivity, it also creates a shared space that transforms the relationship between interviewer and interviewee: "It seems to me, that it doesn't matter how much the subject of the film changes, if I don't change too—if there isn't a kind of chemical reaction between us—then the film loses half its significance" (Gerow and Kore-eda). The chemistry between Kore-eda and his subjects is particularly evident in two documentaries that he filmed in 1993 and 1994 about Hirata Yutaka, the first Japanese national to be diagnosed with AIDS. *This Is How I'm Living with AIDS—Hirata Yutaka Recounts* (*AIDS to ikiru hito—Hirata Yutaka san wa kataru*, 1993) introduces us to the activist, while the second film, *August without Him*, provides a retrospective of the final months before Hirata succumbs to the disease. Over the course of making these two documentaries, the relationship that Kore-eda developed with Hirata transformed him from an objective filmmaker into a participant in Hirata's ongoing story due to a mutual affinity shared between the two that extended beyond their professional relationship. Unattached to a job or family, Hirata moved from place to place, becoming a part of the lives of his large network of acquaintances. Heavily dependent on others around him for support, Hirata manipulated family and friends into assisting him with errands when he lost his mobility and eyesight. He even cajoled Kore-eda and his camera crew into helping him move to a new apartment when they showed up to shoot him one day. In fact, the reason Kore-eda made a second documentary about Hirata is partially due to the codependency between them, as he explained in an early interview:

> After the first [documentary] was finished, Hirata and the film crew (not just me) felt the relationship between us, developed during the shoot, hadn't ended. . . . He hated being alone, understandably so in his condition. The crew couldn't just leave him. That was the impetus for continuing to film. Hirata was a difficult character, very lovable, but selfish and demanding. He saw through people, and got them involved in his life. *August without Him* shows his relationship with the crew. He asked us to film him until he died. But when he was dying in the hospital, he asked me to keep visiting, yet not to film anymore. That was difficult, because, for the crew, there was a great difference between being Hirata's volunteers and shooting the documentary. The film shows our dilemma. (Paletz and Saito 54–55)

The closeness between the two produced real feelings of grief for Kore-eda when Hirata died. Recounting memories of the time they spent together, Kore-eda described the impact of Hirata's death on him: "To me, the image of people confronting the death of loved ones can be beautiful. They have to face death in order to keep living. They have to decide whether to keep memories once shared, or to erase the past. My greatest theme, in documentary and narrative, is how people overcome the violence of a loss and deal with memories that now exist only on one side. I'm among the survivors in *August without Him*" (Paletz and Saito 55).

A breakdown of boundaries between detached filmmaker and subject in Kore-eda's relationship with Sekine Hiroshi, a man with no capacity for short-term memory, reveals the communal dimensions of personal acts of remembering. In *Without Memory*, Kore-eda and his team documented the day-to-day experiences of Sekine, who fell victim to Wernicke-Korsakoff syndrome while recovering from abdominal surgery. This syndrome prevented him from accumulating short-term memories, making him dependent on his wife and two sons to function in daily life. Though the filmmakers initially focused their attention on Sekine and his family in an effort to remain outside the story, they soon realized that they were not just documenting Sekine's efforts to regain his powers of memory but also participating in them. Adam Bingham argues that the documentary uses objective devices such as "voice of God" narration as "smoke-screens" that conceal the attempt of the documentary to problematize the impersonality of the filmmakers (153). Through their periodic visits to tape sessions with Sekine and his family, they became part of the routine of Sekine's life and thus part of his therapy. Though they had to remind Sekine who they were during the first few visits to his home, in the course of subsequent sessions, Sekine started to recognize them, even recalling their names. As Kore-eda and his team participated in Sekine's own process of remembering, they transferred some of the control over documenting the experience to him. Providing Sekine with a video camera, they allowed him to record his own experiences in a gesture that draws connections between filmmaking and memory, connections Kore-eda would develop in features such as *After Life* and *The Truth* and briefly in *Like Father, Like Son*.[10] Although *Without Memory* does not indicate whether Sekine recovers his memory or not, the film-within-a-film structure reveals the way Sekine's life was swallowed up in the acts of remembering those around him, forming a shared space of memory with them. Like film, which has the capacity to carry within itself the basis of other films that can progress over time, this shared space of remembering gives life to acts of recollection that extend beyond the memory function of a single subject. There is not just one master film, one memory, that relays experiences, the documentary suggests; instead, other stories exist as well that develop organically, unconstrained by the artificial boundaries created in film production and in the individual experience of the past.[11] The creation of shared spaces of memory in Kore-eda's feature films will be discussed in the last section of the book.

The lessons Kore-eda learned in making documentaries influenced his approach to feature filmmaking. Accordingly, his process of producing fictional films after *Maborosi* reflects a greater attention to the collaborative energy that emerges on set. As with his documentaries, aspects of nonorganization manifest in the dynamic interaction among Kore-eda, his cast, and his crew. While Kore-eda likes to streamline the number of bodies on location when making documentaries, preferring to work with fewer than ten staff members, this number balloons to around thirty or forty when he makes features, creating ample opportunity for others to share in the creative process (Kubota and Kore-eda 169). Kore-eda acknowledges the collaborative nature of his films in conversation with other directors known for their cooperative approach to moviemaking. In a conversation with Kore-eda, Japanese anime director Hosoda Mamoru (b. 1967) argued that a director cannot claim sole ownership over a final product (Hosoda and Kore-eda 23). Known for creating an open work environment in his Tokyo studio, Hosoda recognizes the contributions of the entire crew and even consumers in creating the popularity of works such as *The Girl Who Leapt through Time* (*Toki wo kakeru shōjo*, 2006), *Summer Wars* (*Samā wōzu*, 2009), and *Mirai* (2018). Anthropologist Ian Condry, who conducted ethnographic research at Hosoda's studio, argues that to truly understand Hosoda's work, it is necessary to look closely at the relationships among individuals at the site of a film's production (2–4). It is the space between the product and people, Condry suggests, where the vibrancy and meaning of the work are located.

In much the same way, Kore-eda's films evolve like living organisms, as the real conditions of the participants' lives and their interactions on set give shape to the scenarios that launch his productions (Kan and Kore-eda 30). Instead of fully formed screenplays, Kore-eda's films often go into production as little more than treatments that he will edit and rewrite several times during filming, allowing room for the film to grow as it is shot (Kore-eda, "Dokyumentari" 81). The production of *Distance*, a film about the aftermath of an act of religious violence that is based on the real-life incident of the Tokyo subway gas attacks in 1995, began with just a series of situations in which actors improvised their lines as they played the part of the bereaved family members of those responsible for the events (Michida and Kore-eda 118). Although Kore-eda Club member Natsukawa Yui, who plays one of the bereaved, initially struggled without a script, other actors suggested that the freedom to improvise scenes allowed them to express their own feelings about a real historical event that profoundly affected all citizens. Kore-eda observes his actors on set, moreover, and customizes his screenplays to fit their mannerisms, often amending lines in response to their idiosyncrasies (Binoche and Kore-eda 169). In the process of shooting *Like Father, Like Son*, Kore-eda revised the script fifty times, editing it almost daily as he worked with actors and grew to understand their temperaments. He followed the same process on the set of *The Truth* (Arai 21), reportedly angering Binoche by repeatedly changing her lines at the last minute (Hori and Kore-eda 30).

In particular, Kore-eda likes to modify his scripts to conform to the unaffected acting style of the many child actors with whom he works. Since first working with schoolchildren on *Lessons from a Calf*, Kore-eda has directed child actors in almost all his features, working particularly closely with them in *Nobody Knows*; *I Wish*; *Like Father, Like Son*; *Shoplifters*; and *The Truth*. Lauded by critics for the way he elicits natural performances from children, Kore-eda acknowledges the respect and affinity he has toward them—an affinity that almost took him in a different career direction as a teacher, if not for his subpar performance in school (Ogawa and Kore-eda 59). As he does with his adult actors, Kore-eda opts for a flexible and open approach to directing children and crafting their lines. In making *Nobody Knows* and *I Wish*, Kore-eda did not give the actors a script. Instead, he provided them with verbal instructions and coaching on the morning of each shoot (Jonze and Kore-eda 47). To provide child actors with the freedom to express themselves on set, he left the plot open, designing the story around the conditions at locations and encouraging his young actors to improvise.

He is not above rewriting entire screenplays to fit the actors he eventually casts. Originally intending *I Wish* to be a "boy meets girl" story, Kore-eda was impressed by the chemistry of the film's two eventual stars—Maeda Kōki and Maeda Ōshiro, a comedy duo of two brothers in real life—and rewrote the treatment as a story about siblings separated by their parents' divorce in order to cast them (Takazaki and Kore-eda 70).

The freedom Kore-eda affords his child actors results in performances that manifest the creative potential of nonorganization. Exploiting children's spontaneity and artlessness, Kore-eda seeks to guide them without overtly directing them. This involves a delicate dance between shaping his actors' performances and allowing his actors to shape the film.[12] He likens this give-and-take style of directing to a "game of catch" (Binoche and Kore-eda 169). Appreciating that "making believe is what [children] do and how they grow" (Rafferty), Kore-eda designs his film sets to allow children to express their imaginations and for this process to be documented on film (Shimamori and Kore-eda 178). He employs an observational style when directing child actors, allowing them to explore new environments on their own terms as the camera tracks them in long takes that often extend beyond the boundaries established by the set and even the diegetic world, organically producing new trajectories of motion. This is particularly the case with *I Wish*, a film in which the main roles are played by children. *I Wish* tells of a family of four divided by divorce. While the father, Kenji, lives with the youngest son, Ryūnosuke, in the northern Kyushu city of Fukuoka, the mother, Nozomi, and the older son, Kōichi, move two hundred miles away to Nozomi's hometown in the southern Kyushu city of Kagoshima. Desperate to reunite the family, Kōichi hatches a plan to meet his brother halfway between the two cities. The opening of a new bullet train line linking the two metropolitan areas, Kōichi believes, may provide an opportunity to unify the family. According to a rumor spread among the kids at Kōichi's elementary school, when the trains pass each other for the first time, a large amount of energy will be released, granting a wish to those who witness it. To capture the boys' adventure, Kore-eda employs a handheld camera to track the children as they dash through busy train stations, rush aboard departing trains, and run through city streets, allowing them to lead him along the way. Many instances of the children's performances—such as the scene in which they sing "Y.M.C.A." together—are reflective not of professional actors playing roles but of actual children (Shigesato and Kore-eda 204). On numerous occasions, Kore-eda allowed the children to explore the city as they made their way to the place where they could watch the trains instead of hurrying the children along. While filming one scene, he patiently waited while the children temporarily got sidetracked by a field of cosmos, and the footage of the children admiring the lavender flowers made its way into the film.

These moments of excess in *I Wish* are echoed in *The Truth*, a film that focuses on a strained relationship between Fabienne, one of the great stars of French cinema, and her daughter, Lumir, a screenwriter living in New York with her American husband, Hank, and her daughter, Charlotte. Even though he was directing some of the greats of French cinema in Binoche and Deneuve, Kore-eda gave equal time to Clémentine Grenier (Charlotte), capturing her performance behind the scenes. As the small family arrives at Fabienne's home, Charlotte carries her luggage up the stairs to her mother's childhood room, in which she will be staying. While the adults talk, the camera follows Charlotte up the stairs, capturing her as she explores her mother's trinkets and toys and puts on an impromptu play. Later, on the set of a new film that Fabienne is shooting, Kore-eda tracks Charlotte as she playfully explores the set,

Figure 3. Charlotte explores her grandmother's film set in *The Truth*.

revealing metacommentary on the way he encourages his own child actors to explore the space of his shooting locations. Although the artificial world of the set was constructed to create a film in which Charlotte's grandmother stars, it is repurposed as a playground for Charlotte in this scene, a place in which her own story unfolds. Without transforming into films for children, Kore-eda's works that utilize this organic approach free children from an adult gaze, providing the audience a glimpse of their world (Kishida and Kore-eda 149).

This attention to the process of filmmaking that develops as a result of the unbounded growth of stories and perspectives demonstrates aspects of nonorganization in Kore-eda's works that creatively conflict with his own propensity as an auteur to control the final product. Drawing on the real experiences and inclinations of his actors, Kore-eda produces his features in a manner that is not entirely different from the way he shoots his documentaries. In both cases, energy generated by interactions among filmmakers, subjects, and actors upsets the boundaries and levels the hierarchies established by the filmmaking process. Just as the relationship Kore-eda develops with his interviewees pulls him into their stories, impromptu performances on the set of his features alter the flow of his films, creating shared spaces of experience and memory in his works. The organizational dynamics of the production of Kore-eda's films provide a framework for looking at the shared spaces of family, community, and memory in his features.

Grifter Families and Networks of Exchange in *Shoplifters*

The boom surrounding the 2018 film *Crazy Rich Asians* by director Jon Chu (b. 1979) reinforces the stereotype of a consumer-happy nouveau riche in Asia. However, another filmic trend of the last few years explores the other side of this glitzy fantasy to expose the hidden reality of economic inequality in East Asia. In contrast to the wealthy families depicted in *Crazy Rich Asians*, the cinematic motif of the "grifter family" in Kore-eda's *Shoplifters* and South Korean director Bong Joon-ho's *Parasite* (*Gisaengchung*, 2019) reveals the struggle of the underclass to survive even in wealthy societies such as Japan and South Korea. This section explores this motif and its function in Kore-eda's experimentation in *Shoplifters* with different forms of communal bodies other than the nuclear model that has served as an appendage to the economic policies of the state. While the film's representation of underprivileged families who are required to beg, borrow, and steal to survive reflects Japan's transition from a society based on the "principle of equality" (*byōdō shugi*) to one built around winners and losers during the last few decades, the film also presents a vision of the family as a networked body, one that revitalizes outdated notions of family in contemporary Japan.

The use of the grifter motif in East Asian cinema speaks to the burdens placed on the family by the managed economies of South Korea and Japan. Though the process and timing of development differ between these nations, they have shared a similar path to rapid economic growth under the East Asian model of state-sponsored capitalism. To realize growth, both these traditions placed enormous burdens on individual families, a unit of society often identified as the basis of national development. In South Korea, economic growth in the 1980s and 1990s was spurred by government support of chaebol, large, family-run corporations that formed in the 1950s. The growth of chaebol at the top of society diminished economic opportunities for families at the other end of the spectrum, who were nevertheless expected to dedicate their efforts to the national goals of economic progress. Bong's *Parasite* demonstrates the weight placed on these disadvantaged families, who were expected to sacrifice for the larger good. The film involves two domestic units separated by class: the wealthy Parks, who live in a fancy house at the top of a hill in Seoul, and the aspirational Kims, who live in a half-basement at the bottom. The Kims swindle their way into the Parks' home, taking jobs as servants—positions that they must violently seize from the previous housekeeper and her husband, who faithfully served the Parks for years despite living in poverty. Because conventional means of social mobility are limited in the top-down economic society depicted in the film, underprivileged families like the Kims are forced to fight tooth and nail to advance in a system in which their service and loyalty go unrewarded.

The grifter motif in *Shoplifters* is a response to the pressure placed on the family to act as a primary source of security for the nation's development. According to Michel Foucault, the family was co-opted for the purposes of economic progress in First World countries: "The organization of the 'conventional family' came to be regarded . . . as an

indispensable instrument of political control and economic regulation"
(122). Even though the *ie* system (the organization of national house-
holds during the prewar and interwar years) was abolished as part of
the reforms under the US occupation of Japan (1945–52) after World
War II, the feudal characteristics of the family lived on through the
patrilineal organization of the postwar family system. Consisting of a
hierarchical relationship of a breadwinner father, a homemaker mother,
and children bound by blood ties, the ideal postwar family was expected
to serve as the foundational unit of society and to bear the burden of
national progress (Ishii-Kuntz 200–01). Under neoliberal policy, for
instance, the family was considered a substitute for the welfare state
(Kingston 60–61). Japan's social safety net, which enabled the nation's
economic development, was outsourced to families by the policies of
the Liberal Democratic Party (LDP), the main ruling coalition of Japan
from 1955 to the present.[13] Families were expected to relieve the nation
of the economic weight of providing welfare to its citizens by taking care
of their own. However, the recession of the 1990s and 2000s led to the
weakening of the very family units on which the government depended,
as many of the benefits that sustained workers and their families were
reduced in the widespread corporate downsizing of the time. As lifetime
employment guarantees at companies dried up, traditional breadwinners
were no longer able to support dependents, leading to the destabilization
of family units through an increase in divorce rates and other disruptions
to domestic life.

Notwithstanding the weakening of the family by the recession, even
greater weight was placed on this foundational unit of society to pull
Japan out of its economic slide during the first two decades of the 2000s.
The government looked to individuals and families to assume more
responsibility in supporting the social infrastructure that had allowed
the nation to realize global economic superiority in the 1980s (Kingston
60–61). Prime Minister Koizumi stressed the importance of personal
responsibility in helping the nation recover. Proposed changes to the
constitution by the LDP in 2012, moreover, underscored the centrality
of the family to the economic well-being of the nation. Recommended
revisions of "Chapter III: The Rights and Duties of the People" reinforced the mandate for families to secure the national safety net by add-
ing the phrase "members of the family must help each other" (Matsui).

Despite the destabilization of traditional domestic units during the last few decades, then, the state has continued to look to the family to ensure the economic viability of the nation.

Kore-eda's films thematize the pressure placed on the family to act as a national safety net. In a conversation with Kore-eda, writer Takeda Satetsu suggested that many of Kore-eda's films, including *After the Storm*, critique the ideal family imagined in the revision of chapter 3 of the constitution by depicting the problems facing real families (Takeda and Kore-eda 254). Indeed, his visual narratives feature domestic units that do not conform to the prototypical view of the family as the corner-stone of the nation envisioned by the LDP, including families disrupted by divorce (*I Wish, After the Storm, Our Little Sister*), parental aban-donment (*Nobody Knows, Shoplifters*, and *Broker*), death (*Maborosi, Distance*, and *Still Walking*), and even children switched at birth (*Like Father, Like Son*). *After the Storm*, for instance, portrays the way Japan placed the burden of its economic development on individual family units that make up the larger nation. The top-down order of both the normative family and the larger social system of which these domestic units, both overseen by men, are a part in the film leads to exploitation within the relationships that make up these systems, as those above often profit from those below in the social hierarchy. Toiling away in the fam-ily's small apartment in a large *danchi*—the symbol of the mobilization of the family for national economic goals—Yoshiko's constricted lifestyle in the film is due to the profligate ways of her late husband, who mort-gaged the long-term security of the family for immediate gratification, pawning family heirlooms to pay off gambling debts. Ryōta inherited his father's squandering ways. Fifteen years ago, he won the Shimao Toshio literary award for his debut novel—a work he wrote by stealing family secrets—but has had little success since. In the years following his debut, Ryōta became a gambler like his father, pilfering money and valuables from his mother's modest apartment to finance trips to the racetrack. As a private investigator, he profits from the failure of the family: disgruntled husbands and wives hire him to surveil their spouses to better position themselves in divorce settlements, while he blackmails the guilty parties with photographic evidence of their infidelity, making money from both sides of the exchange. Farther up the ladder, Ryōta's boss also benefits from these illicit activities, requiring Ryōta to kick up a portion of the money that he takes from these scams. In this way, the family unit bears the burden of the profiteering performed by those in powerful positions within the family and society. The plundering of this foundational unit by people in power has weakened its structural integrity and compromised its ability to stabilize the nation.

Shoplifters, a film about a makeshift clan of six who make ends meet through petty theft, goes beyond Kore-eda's earlier films in drawing attention to the burdens placed on families.[14] Featuring a clan of unrelated grifters not only questions the primacy of blood relationships as the determining factor of the cohesion of the family unit but also takes aim at the myth of the universal middle class and the mandate of personal responsibility at the basis of LDP policies. Having slipped through the cracks of Japan's managed society, characters in *Shoplifters* defy the myth of a robust middle class by working hourly positions in blue-collar industries, occupying spaces that the government does not want to acknowledge: the sex shops and gambling parlors filled with unemployed, lonely people who struggle to make ends meet.[15] It is not enough, however, for *Shoplifters* to present the Shibatas simply as part of the working class; this would still designate for them a place within the stratified order. A family that struggles to make ends meet can be appropriated into a narrative of self-reliance that positions the domestic unit as part of the social safety net. This is the case with Yoshiko in *After the Storm*, who, despite subsisting on a meagre pension, lives within her means while maintaining her family network. *Shoplifters*, on the other hand, humanizes folks on the outside of the social order, those who do not contribute to the economic well-being of the nation, according to LDP policies. By stealing, the family is neither taking responsibility for their own needs nor providing a foundation for the larger national collective; they are, instead, an unproductive part of the system. The use of unproductive criminals as main characters in the film rubbed many the wrong way in Japan, including former prime minister Abe, who famously refused to congratulate Kore-eda on winning the Palme d'Or for *Shoplifters* in a tacit show of disapproval for the film. However, by forcing viewers to accept characters who are lazy, unscrupulous, and even dishonest, *Shoplifters* resists idealized expectations imposed on them by the mandate of personal responsibility, one that requires even the most disadvantaged to deny their humanity and sacrifice for the nation. The depiction of flawed individuals like these requires that both Kore-eda and his viewers do not pass judgment on even the most irredeemable characters in his films, like the mother who abandons her children in *Nobody Knows*. Rather, critics suggest, Kore-eda's films invite us to consider the forces that come to bear on individuals and families under the demands of the state rather than judge them (Saitō and Kore-eda 138). The humanization of those outside the system in *Shoplifters*, then, underscores the unrealistically onerous burdens placed on families to provide the foundation for national progress.

However, this section is not concerned with reading *Shoplifters* as a critique of economic policy in Japan. Rather, the focus is on the way in which *Shoplifters* and other Kore-eda films revitalize the overcoded institution of the family by visualizing the formation of domestic bodies that develop spontaneously and idiosyncratically in the nexus of government control and neoliberal deregulation. The film humanizes the Shibatas, I suggest, by figuring them through images of nonorganization that inevitably emerge amid the tension among the efforts to regulate families through top-down government policy while forcing them to survive in a world defined by free-market principles. The Shibatas represent the product of these social and economic forces: they conform to traditional markers that designate domestic units in Japan and other First World nations while resisting them at the same time. According to Claude Lévi-Strauss, the contemporary notion of the family implies the following three designations: "The family originates in marriage; it includes the husband, wife, and the children born of their union; and the members of the family are united by legal bonds" (39). Although the Shibatas resemble a normal family of six on the surface, because they are not bound by the same order imposed on those related by blood, the group takes shape organically from the ground up. Osamu, a day laborer; his partner, Nobuyo, a part-time employee at a local laundry; Aki, a sex worker in her early twenties; Shōta, a juvenile boy whom Osamu and Nobuyo find living in an abandoned car; and Yuri, a young victim of parental neglect, gravitate to one another out of mutual benefit. The family lives together with an elderly woman named Hatsue, who owns the home in which they temporarily reside and supports the clan with her government pension—a plot point based on real-life incidents of people stealing the pensions of their deceased parents (Todoroki et al.

19). Osamu and Nobuyo are not married, and Hatsue, whom Aki refers to as "grandma" throughout the film, is not her biological grandmother. Aki's father is the son of Hatsue's late husband and another woman. Out of a sense of responsibility for Hatsue, Aki's father regularly gives money to Hatsue, though it is revealed at the end of the film that Aki's parents, or at least her father, are aware that Aki is living with Hatsue and that the money they give to Hatsue is to compensate her for caring for their daughter.

Resisting conformity with the normative family model, however, the Shibatas represent a superfluous presence in Japan's managed society in the same way that thieves represent an excess of desire in capitalist exchange. As a superfluous presence, the Shibatas are a product of the coding of desire not only through top-down regulation but also by desires that extend beyond this organized system. Since the family is not bound by the strictures that define a traditional domestic unit in Japan, their interactions are not always dictated by the hierarchical order that structures the normative family and regulates its libidinal economy. Indeed, desire escapes the rigid boundaries that designate official families in the film. As we learn, Osamu and Nobuyo are not married but are part of an illicit relationship, having killed Nobuyo's abusive husband in a crime of passion years earlier. Incestuous desire, which is normally suppressed within the hierarchical order of the nuclear family, moreover, spills over in the film when Shōta ogles his "sister" Aki's breasts during a trip to the beach, as we see in a shot / reverse shot of Shōta and a close-up of Aki's chest that dismembers her body with his gaze.

This surplus of desire is reflected in moments of excess in the narrative. The Shibatas' habit of collecting new members stretches the bounds of the normative family and their domicile in frame-within-frame shots filled with bodies lounging in Hatsue's small living room. These shots recall the bustling bodies of the children that fill the camera frame in *Nobody Knows*, a film in which a single mother of four must sneak her family into a small apartment in which she and her oldest son are the only ones approved to live. Smuggled into the apartment in a suitcase, Satoru, the youngest son, bursts out of his cramped confines when his mother opens the suitcase.

The superfluous bodies in both *Shoplifters* and *Nobody Knows*, moreover, are captured as the camera lingers on scenes of family

Figure 4. The bodies of the Shibata family fill the frame and the room in this deep-focus shot from *Shoplifters*.

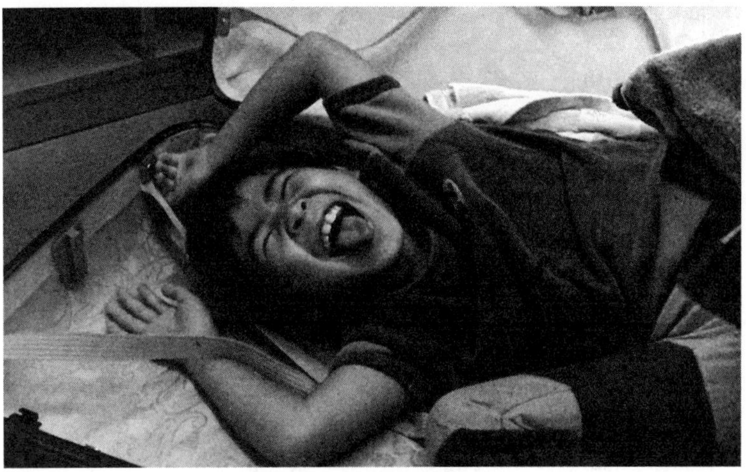

Figure 5. Satoru bursts free from the suitcase in *Nobody Knows*.

intimacy unconcerned about how the moments serve the telos of the story. Free from the concerns of work, Osamu spends a copious amount of time with Shōta and Yuri. The camera tracks the three as they amble along a riverbed path after stealing fishing rods at a local sporting goods store, in no hurry to get home. Later, when Shōta grows resentful of

Yuri's presence in the family and hides in an abandoned car, not unlike
the one in which Osamu and Nobuyo found him years earlier, a wide
shot captures Osamu playfully chasing Shōta in a large, empty parking
lot—their own personal playground—when he comes to take Shōta
home. Images of overflowing bodies in these films, then, represent the
excesses of nonorganization that inevitably spring forth from the organized systems that surround the characters.

As a superfluous presence in society, the Shibatas also figure as an
organic gathering of bodies that collectively seeks to navigate and survive the market economy. Together they create an *assemblage* formed
through forces of nonorganization rather than by a preexisting organizing
framework imposed from above. Deleuze and Guattari use the term
assemblage to describe the self-organizing function of individual parts
within larger systems, parts that are not always already defined in organic
unity (Nail 23). In contrast to the set nature of a *unity*, an assemblage is
a transitory, conditional collection of parts unfixed in their relation to one
another. Deleuze and Guattari liken the components of a unity to pieces
of a puzzle, which are designed to fit together, and the components of
an assemblage to the rocks in a drystone wall, which are not preshaped
by an overarching design and are held in place along "diverging lines"
(*What* 23). In her discussion of the boundaries of embodiment, Margrit
Shildrick comments on the lack of a unifying essence for assemblages:
"In assemblages, it is the connection between disparate components
that produces meaning rather than the other way around, where the
fixed meaning of an element would prescribe the nature of its possible
connections. . . . In other words, there is no internal necessity to the
assemblage, just a set of contingent relations that evolve and change
over time" ("Why" 21).

Because their relationships are not always already defined as a unity,
moreover, individuals can be *deterritorialized*, or subtracted from assemblages, and *reterritorialized* as components of new groups, creating a
constellation of parts that are continually changing while transforming
the larger wholes of which they are a part.

Assemblages like the Shibata family manifest a body of networked
relationships that takes shape amid the wild swings of the market economy. According to Helga Leitner and Eric Sheppard, networks are a
product of stiff competition within market economies; they are a way for

businesses and other organizations to survive when it is tough to make it alone amid the cutthroat competition of global capitalism (148–50). Like assemblages, networks are based in shifting associations rather than enduring essences: "The conditions of possibility and actions of network participants are defined by their relationship with other participants, rather than by their own inherent characteristics" (149). Leitner and Sheppard describe these relationships within networks with five important characteristics:

> [First,] networks evolve a relational organizational structure that is bottom-up, rather than externally imposed. . . . [S]econd, networks are *collaborative*. . . . Third, networks are nonhierarchical. Network participants are linked by two-way, horizontal relationships that give each participant a voice over the collective outcome. Fourth, networks are flexible. Two aspects of flexibility are typically invoked: (1) network linkages are continually subject to change, and network structures are periodically restructured; (2) network boundaries are fuzzy: participants can leave the networks and potential participants can join. Fifth, the spatiality of networks is topological. By this, we mean that networks evolve by creating linkages between participants who were not previously connected. (150)

The collaborative, nonhierarchical, and flexible nature of self-organizing networks, then, allows them to "minimize the destructive aspects of market-based competition and encourage collaboration by facilitating tacit mutuality and trust between participants" (Leitner and Sheppard 150). As a self-organizing network, the Shibata family provides for the needs of its individual members by virtue of its shifting and flexible structure. Divorce, death, unemployment, and other domestic issues represented in the film both simulate and result from the turbulence of the market economy, leading to the breakdown of the traditional domestic unit and the rise of temporary connections that are formed for the mutual benefit of individual members.

Self-organizing networks are better equipped to handle the enduring challenges of a society based on winners and losers under capitalist hegemony. Because they are susceptible to downsizing and job-related injuries, manual laborers struggle to serve as the primary breadwinners for the family; thus, their spouses are often required to work part-time as well (Roberson 128). To ensure the survival of blue-collar workers in a social system in which employment is not guaranteed, the Shibata network includes three breadwinners: Osamu, Nobuyo, and Aki. This configuration proves consequential when both Osamu and Nobuyo lose their jobs for a period of time: Osamu is injured while working as a day laborer, and Nobuyo is laid off when her coworker blackmails her, forcing her to reject a job for which both are in competition. The family also relies on Hatuse, who provides the home in which the family lives, as well as money from her pension. These multiple sources of income create a unit more stable than one dependent on a single breadwinner. What is more, this collective can deterritorialize and reterritorialize with ease, regularly reconfiguring to deal with the vicissitudes of life. Indeed, seemingly artificial plot devices in Kore-eda's films, like child-switching at birth in *Like Father, Like Son* (although the incident really did happen), are also presented as a way to simulate the many ways a family can be disrupted within a market economy. New members—for example, Yuri, whom the family finds neglected on her porch one evening—can easily join the temporary collective, while other members can depart if conditions necessitate. For example, Shōta deliberately sabotages an attempted shoplifting to protect Yuri and afterward gets injured and apprehended by the police. This turn of events sets in motion the scattering of the family. The police arrest Nobuyo after they discover Hatsue's body buried in her home. They send Yuri back to her legal family and place Shōta in state custody. We do not see what happens to Aki, though it is assumed that she becomes independent (or returns to live with her family) after Hatsue passes away. Yet just as quickly as the Shibatas' network dissolves, it regenerates in a different form as Osamu and Shōta's relationship is renewed even as the two are forced to live separately.[16]

As a product of the market economy, then, the network that keeps the Shibatas together is based on the principle of exchange. Their interactions as a family are not a manifestation of a communal alternative to the capitalist system; instead, they are defined by the idea of exchange itself—the trading of financial resources for emotional support. Osamu and Nobuyo depend on Hatsue for things that they lack, including a house in which to live, and they provide the widow with the companionship she needs. Living in Hatsue's home, Aki, Shōta, and Yuri all find the love and intimacy that they were lacking in their previous situations, while they provide Hatsue with an extended family with whom she can spend her last days. With Hatsue's death at the end of the film, we learn that this is not the first time Osamu and Nobuyo have lived with an elderly woman to whom they provided companionship in exchange for monetary resources. The very idea of exchange dictates the dynamics within the Shibata family, highlighting the way the collective does not stand outside the larger economic forces of the family's environment.

As the Shibatas demonstrate, the emotional connection that develops among members of a group that live together out of choice rather than mere blood relationships revitalizes the symbolic order of the normative family, a static system into which members are appropriated before they are even born, preinscribed as a child or sibling while still in the womb (Althusser 77). The temporary nature of the Shibatas' "found family" in both a hereditary and a legal sense necessitates that the Shibatas must continually renew their connections to one another by creating rituals and sign systems that are unique to them. Rather than depend on the names and rituals that they inherit as part of a familial unity defined by the society and the state, the Shibatas formulate their own sign systems through everyday interactions. Throughout the film, Osamu continually prompts Shōta to refer to him as his "dad" and to Yuri as his "sister." Though these are the same identifiers utilized within official familial units bound by blood, they have nevertheless been stripped of an official function, becoming, first and foremost, terms of affection. Highlighting the importance of naming in group bonding, the family christens Yuri "Rin" to conceal her identity and initiate her as part of the family. But even as it acknowledges the power of shared genetics in connecting fam-ily members, *Shoplifters* also focuses on traits that result from shared rituals and trauma rather than heredity. While taking a bath together, Nobuyo and Yuri compare similar scars on their arms, which reveal a shared history of abuse rather than physical manifestations of heredity. Likewise, Osamu teaches Shōta how to steal in a local grocery store, passing on the family business to his "son." Later, Shōta tutors Yuri in the same techniques as the young girl is inducted into the family. Kore-eda discusses the way the shared ritual of shoplifting unites the Shibatas as a clan: "I read about families that would shoplift together. Now—I don't know whether they were blood-related or not, but it was a news item that talked about how the whole family was shoplifting. What held this family together is the crime. They were held together out of a sense of duty to commit this crime together. In that sense, I read these articles and that's what inspired me" (Chang).

The visual representation of the Shibatas depicts the growth of this nonorganized family. Notwithstanding their lack of the markers that designate traditional domestic units, the framing of the family together creates a sense of both anonymity and intimacy. Outside of the home, the members are captured through static long shots that isolate them from others, highlighting their individuality. In scenes captured inside Hatsue's small house, Kore-eda framed and blocked the characters as a group, capturing their interactions. The film opens during the winter, when cold temperatures force the clan to huddle together in the living room to take advantage of shared body heat. Bodies fill the frame in deep-focus shots of the close quarters of the room, while close-ups with a handheld camera capture the intimacy and immediacy of their relationships as the family members banter with one another over meals. They are not the abstractions of poor people created through media stories but real, live individuals. Kore-eda captured characters' hands and feet in both *Shoplifters* and *Nobody Knows* to represent them as anonymous and forgotten while humanizing them at the same time. Kore-eda suggested in a conversation with Hosoda, who is also known for depicting hands to represent his characters, that showing a character's hands or feet can often be more intimate than revealing their face (Hosoda and Kore-eda 19). As it does in much of Japanese cinema, everyday life unfolds against the changing seasons. Characters share the culinary treats of each part of the year: hotpot and rice cakes in the winter and cold noodles and ice pops in the summer. A high-angle shot almost at bird's-eye perspective captures the family watching fireworks on their porch during the heat of the summer. Framed between the roof of the house and the trees in their yard, the Shibatas are united in an image that also depicts the way in which they have slipped through the cracks of society. Much like the small apartment in which the children in *Nobody Knows* while away their days, Hatsue's old house is framed as a forgotten space in the jungle of newer condominiums that surround it.

Blocking and framing are the tools by which Kore-eda composes familial assemblages from the ground up in films such as *Still Walking*.

Figure 6. The Shibatas fall through the cracks in society as captured in this bird's-eye shot in *Shoplifters*.

In the film, which primarily takes place over the course of one day, the surviving members of the Yokoyama family, including the father, Kyōhei; mother, Toshiko; second son, Ryōta, who recently married a widow, Yukari, with a young son named Atsushi; and daughter, Chinami, gather at the end of the summer during the Obon holiday to commemorate the death of the eldest son, Junpei, who drowned saving a distressed swimmer twelve years earlier. During the opening scenes, a series of two- and three-shots of the Yokoyamas demonstrates the emotional and genetic divisions that exist among individuals who come together as a larger family. Captured in a sequence of three-shots that frames the new unit together, Ryōta, Yukari, and Atsushi travel to the Yokoyama home by train. This sequence is crosscut with a scene captured by a two-shot of the matriarch of the Yokoyama family, Toshiko, sitting in her kitchen with her daughter, Chinami, preparing food as they wait for Ryōta and his new family to arrive. In a family restaurant at the station, a lateral two-shot of Ryōta and Yukari having a drink suggests that they are in no hurry to unite with the rest of the family. Atsushi, busy at first getting a refill at the bar, joins them to create a dirty two-shot, with Atsushi and Yukari framed by half of Ryōta's torso, suggesting a family that is still in the process of bonding. When Yukari leaves, Ryōta and Kyōhei are left at the table. The awkward nature of their new relationship as stepfather and stepson is illustrated through a series of over-the-shoulder shots that highlight their lack of connection as Ryōta struggles to start a conversation with his son.

When Ryōta and his family finally arrive at the Yokoyama home, additional bodies added to the scene create an awkward impression at first. Yukari enters the frame that captures Toshiko and Chinami in the kitchen, forming an uncomfortable three-shot that indicates her outsider status as a new member of the family. As the Yokoyamas gather in the living room overlooking the backyard, a camera set up outside the home pictures the family in a crowd shot at an angle that positions characters separately from each other, highlighting the lack of rapport among them. It is not until later, when everyone sits down at the family table, that we see them framed as one unit. Captured from the same camera distance outside the house, the sliding doors that earlier divided the characters serve as a frame that draws them together. This pattern is repeated throughout the film as the camera depicts family members who, at first uncomfortable with each other, eventually share the frame in a more natural way. In contrast to the shot / reverse shots that captured Ryōta and Kyōhei's interaction early in the film, a two-shot captures them taking a bath together according to customs of father-and-son bonding.

Figure 7. Yukari struggles to enter the frame and the family in this shot from *Still Walking*.

The assemblages Kore-eda visualizes in his films revitalize traditional notions of family by developing new lines of connection other than the patrilineal ones formed through hierarchy and preserved through male inheritance. They create systems of familial continuity that are not determined by either feudalistic traditions or the top-down logic of the state. The rupturing of the patriarchal line in *Still Walking* through death leads to the formation of networks formed out of necessity that allow for the survival of tradition. In the film, the lines of patriarchal inheritance that flow from father to son are disrupted by the death of Junpei years earlier, who was expected to take over his father's medical practice, which is run out of the Yokoyama family home. With second son Ryōta, an underemployed art restorer, unable to take over the clinic, no one will assume the practice once Kyōhei is gone. The severing of blood ties leads to tension between Ryōta and his father, who is concerned about his legacy. In place of a system of inheritance based on blood ties, the family regenerates through flexible relationships that serve expedient needs. Despite not being related to Kyōhei by blood, Atsushi is encouraged by Kyōhei to follow in his shoes when the young boy wanders into his clinic and shows interest in medicine.

In *Like Father, Like Son*, two nuclear families headed by separate patriarchs form a networked relationship between the two domestic units. The film is based on real incidents of baby switching that transpired during the 1960s in Japan and is influenced by the book *The Baby Switching Incident: 17 Years of Broken Bonds* (*Akachan torichigae jiken no 17 nen no nejireta kizuna*, 2002). *The Baby Switching Incident* recounts one incident of baby switching in Okinawa in which the two affected families sought to collaborate in raising both children instead of cutting off ties with each other after they switched their children back (Todoroki and Kinbara 60). Just like most families who were victims of baby switching, the Nonomiyas and Saikis in *Like Father, Like Son* initially decide to raise their biological children separately. However, even after the exchange, the two mothers regularly consult about childcare and the particularities of the children they raised from birth. Unable to reconcile their emotional attachments with their new reality, the families gravitate toward a more open-ended relationship by the end of the film, though we never see it materialize completely. Film critic Todoroki Yukio suggested in a conversation with Kinbara Yuka that *Like Father,*

Like Son ends without a clear preference for either the continuity of the single-family system bound by blood or a "commune" model, in which the division between the families breaks down (60).

Patriarchal authority is supplanted by matriarchal and sororal lines in Kore-eda's films. The patrilineal organization is discarded completely in *Our Little Sister* in favor of a sororal tradition, one that forms the foundation and continuity of the family name and home. The film focuses on the lives of three sisters from the Kōda family—Sachi, Yoshino, and Chika—who were left to raise themselves after their parents' divorce. When their father had a baby with another woman, their mother left the family and moved to Hokkaido. After years of living on their own in their grandmother's seaside house, the sisters reunite with their adolescent half-sister, Suzu, whose birth led to their parents' divorce. The discovery of their younger sister raises painful memories of the dissolution of their own family years earlier. Yet the three sisters nevertheless forge a connection to Suzu, inviting her to live with them in their grandmother's house—a character itself in the film—which they receive through inheritance (Fukuoka and Kore-eda 215). Unconcerned with joining another family register through marriage, the sisters form a familial network that grows out of a patriarchal line but is not bound to it. This network is based on the exchange of physical support—the sisters share household chores and collectively bring in income—and on rituals of bonding. Even though Suzu is not related to the side of the family that owns the home by blood, she becomes part of the sisters' house by living in it and participating in the family's tradition of making plum sake.[17]

Instead of directly critiquing policies that rely on the normative family to stabilize the nation, Kore-eda's films concern themselves with the new types of families that have emerged in response to these forces. The choice not to tie up loose ends and restore the cohesion of the traditional family resists the ideological function of closure in narrative cinema, allowing families to develop organically beyond the parameters of plot or political ideology. The blending of the traditional markers of family—physical traits—with newly developed rituals in Kore-eda's films acknowledges the feudalistic nature of the family while also allowing room for its ongoing reconstitution. Figuring as a surplus of desire in the regulation of social and domestic life, the family that emerges in *Shoplifters* and in many of Kore-eda's other films is a product of both this system and the moments when communal experience extends beyond these rigid limitations, manifesting as both organized and nonorganized bodies in response to the challenges of everyday life within the neoliberal social order.

Reimagining Masculine Bodies in *Hana*; *Like Father, Like Son*; and *The Third Murder*

This section explores the representation of masculinity in Kore-eda's films in greater depth, analyzing the way Kore-eda uses his work to reimagine bodies that have traditionally been defined as an extension of corporate and state control. *Like Father, Like Son* and *The Third Murder* rework traditional notions of manhood presented in film and in society, including the dominant male archetype of postwar Japan, the "feudal father," who served as the "main pillar" (*daikoku bashira*) of the household from the 1950s to the early 1990s. Under the logic of the nation's managed economy, the feudal father was epitomized in the "salaryman," or the ubiquitous white-collar corporate worker. A construct of state capitalism, the salaryman was conceived as both a loyal employee to a corporation and the head of his own nuclear family unit (Roberson and Suzuki 8). The "ideal hegemonic sense of masculinity," Masako Ishii-Kuntz suggests, manifests through the salaryman's role as the breadwinner for the family (199). Under this model, men served their families and their larger nation by devoting their energy to companies (Mathews 116). However, with the recession of the 1990s, salarymen lost many of the benefits that came with unwavering loyalty to their companies, including the "three treasures" that were traditionally promised to corporate workers: lifetime employment, a seniority system, and unionism. The diminishing importance of salarymen in recent decades has led to the decentering of the feudal father archetype in the Japanese cultural consciousness as other expressions of masculinity have emerged to take its place (Roberson 127).

Kore-eda's films seek to move beyond the feudal father archetype and the traditional values at its core. As somewhat of an anomaly in his oeuvre, his fifth feature film, *Hana: The Tale of the Reluctant Samurai*, provides a reworking of the archetype in an actual feudal context. Unlike most of Kore-eda's films, which take place in contemporary times, *Hana* is Kore-eda's one and only period piece, set during the Edo period in Japan (1600–1868). The story centers on an unproven samurai named Sōzaemon (played by Okada Jun'ichi) who moves to the slums of Edo (now Tokyo) to restore honor to his family and clan by killing the man who killed his father. This plot line references one of Japan's most treasured tales, a central text for the expression of feudal values: *The Treasury of Loyal Retainers (Chūshingura)*, the fictionalized account of a real historical incident involving forty-seven masterless samurai and their efforts to avenge the death of their master. In 1701 a high-ranking local lord named Asano disgraced himself by drawing his sword on the master of ceremony, an official named Kira, at a reception held in the capital. Although the exact reason for the attempted assault is unknown, it is assumed that Asano was provoked by an insult by Kira. As a consequence of this disgraceful act, Asano was ordered to commit *seppuku* (ritual disembowelment), while Kira got off with no punishment. Two years after the incident, in 1703, forty-seven of Asano's retainers, who had become masterless samurai due to the death of their lord, avenged their master by invading Kira's mansion, killing him, and placing his decapitated head on Asano's grave. Turning themselves over to authorities, they were all ordered to commit *seppuku*, which they did together on the same day in a collective expression of self-sacrifice. In celebration of this ultimate act of duty, honor, and loyalty, the story of the forty-seven samurai has been memorialized in Japanese literature and theater through fictionalized accounts of *The Treasury of Loyal Retainers*, a source text for numerous film and television adaptations. Though briefly banned during the occupation of Japan by US forces after World War II due to its promotion of antidemocratic values, the story has become an enduring legend in Japanese culture.

As a work of historical fiction, however, *Hana* rejects the feudal values of loyalty and family honor expressed in *The Treasury of Loyal Retainers*. Much like his referencing of the style of Ozu and Naruse in his films, in *Hana* Kore-eda draws upon his audience's familiarity with the source text and the genre conventions of samurai cinema in general. He self-consciously installs the same wipe transitions made famous by Kurosawa, one of the most celebrated directors of samurai films, and even incorporates the historical events surrounding *The Treasury of Loyal Retainers* by including the forty-seven masterless samurai as characters in the film, living in the same slums as Sōzaemon as they prepare their attack on Kira. Yet Sōzaemon is anything but a prototypical samurai bent on revenge. He is a hapless fighter hesitant to avenge his father just because he is bound by blood. A gentle soul, Sōzaemon instead teaches the adults and children of the town how to read and write, befriending a young fatherless boy, for whom he becomes a father figure. Instead of connecting to his father through revenge, moreover, he teaches the younger generation the game of go, a game his father taught him how to play. Through a self-conscious treatment of this samurai tale, then, Kore-eda reworks the feudal father archetype by drawing focus away from traditional notions of masculinity.

Using a romantic protagonist in *Hana*, one who seemingly stands outside his historical moment, Kore-eda speaks to present-day concerns. He claims that the story about a warrior hesitant to avenge the death of a loved one was a reaction to the anger in First World nations that surrounded the terrorist attacks of 9/11 (Kore-eda, "Nichijyō" 238). But it is also clear that *Hana* is a way for Kore-eda to interrogate the traditional views of masculinity that manifest in the salaryman archetype, the inheritor of the legacy of the feudal father. Kore-eda's films challenge the basis of the authority of the traditional masculine identity and the bounded integrity of his body in his position as a loyal company worker and the head of a family unit bound by blood relationships. One of Kore-eda's other films, *Like Father, Like Son*, introduces a problem that upsets the hegemony of blood in determining the basis of domestic units (Fukuoka and Kore-eda 197). The film focuses on two families, the Nonomiyas and Saikis, who discover that their eight-year-old sons, Keita and Ryûsei, were switched at birth. This realization upsets the autonomy of the protagonist of the film, Nonomiya Ryōta, who lives in a world in which his masculinity is linked to power and influence. "Although the phallus and penis are discrete terms," Kaja Silverman reminds us, "the later gains its symbolic value from the former" (216).

Living in a postsalaryman age, Ryōta nevertheless performs the identity he inherited through tradition, seeking influence by virtue of his prominent position within two central institutions of society, the corporation and the family.[18] To play Ryōta and the lawyer protagonist of *The Third Murder*, Shigemori Tomoaki, Kore-eda cast singer-songwriter Fukuyama Masaharu, whose tall frame and stylish features reflect the alpha male archetype. Ryōta enjoys a level of prestige in society as an architect at a prominent firm, continually boasting to others about how essential he is to his company. The Nonomiyas' high-rise condo at the center of Tokyo presents a stark contrast to the Saikis' humble home in the back of an electronic storefront on the outskirts of town, calling to mind the distance in Kurosawa Akira's 1962 film *High and Low* (*Tengoku to jigoku*, 1962) between the rich protagonist, who lives in a large house on the top of a hill, and those of a lower socioeconomic level at the bottom of the hill (Todoroki and Kinbara 58). Ryōta's influence is based on his accumulation of resources within this society of exchange—he utilizes his wealth and professional network to solve problems, calling on a lawyer friend to handle legal negotiations with the hospital in which the children were switched. With his aggressive autonomy, Ryōta also represents the entrepreneurial subject fashioned as the main actor in neoliberal economies: "Neoliberalism also stands for a new type of reason and a new kind of production of subjects, which makes it much more than a mere set of economic policies. Subjectivities and social relations are remade according to entrepreneurial patterns. Contemporary neoliberal rationality 'configures human beings exhaustively as market actors; always, only, and everywhere'" (Cercel 3).

Ryōta's prominence within his professional networks translates to his authority within the home. The nature of his position in the hierarchical corporation is reflected in his interactions with his family. He treats his wife and son like employees, giving Keita a "mission" to adjust to his new home with the Saikis. Because Ryōta's influence is caught up in the logic of accumulating and exchanging resources, even relationships become a transaction for him—he is accused of trying to buy family members, offering to acquire both Keita and Ryûsei from the Saikis because he believes both boys would be better off in a home that is financially secure. His positioning within the camera frame, accordingly, reflects an autonomous body at the center of a circumscribed family unit under his control. Ryōta's role as the pillar of the family, supporting his wife and child, manifests through blocking. When Ryōta enters the condominium after work in a scene early in this film, he is framed in the center of the room in a deep-focus shot, taking a seat at the dinner table while his wife and son move around him. Ryōta's dominance in scenes outside the home, moreover, reflects his sovereign control over his family. At the start of the film, Ryōta; his wife, Midori; and Keita meet with administrators from Keita's school. In a shot / reverse shot between school officials and the Nonomiyas, the family is captured in a wide three-shot seated together with Ryōta on the left side of the frame and Midori on the right. The bodies of the two parents frame the much smaller figure of Keita seated in the middle. The framing of the family,

Figure 8. Ryōta is framed as the pillar of the family in *Like Father, Like Son*.

Figure 9. Ryōta is framed as the pillar of the family in *Like Father, Like Son*.

captured head-on in this scene, suggests the orchestration of family portraits, foreshadowing a scene later in the film when the Nonomiyas and Saikis pose for a photo right before switching children. The three members of the family, all in formal black attire, are spaced evenly between each other as three autonomous bodies that form a unit, with the largest of the three bodies, Ryōta, serving as the dominant presence and spokesperson of the family. A cut to a three-shot taken from the side reveals Ryōta's centrality, as the shallow focus on his position in the background allows him to stand out, obscuring the bodies of Midori and Keita in the foreground.

However, the film reworks traditional views of masculinity by disrupting the integrity of the larger bodies that give the phallus its symbolic influence and the male body its autonomy: the family and the corporation. This disruption does not occur through a dismantling of these institutions or through the decentering of Ryōta's position within their organizational structures, like the protagonist of Kurosawa Kiyoshi's *Tokyo Sonata* (*Tōkyō Sonata*, 2008), whose loss of employment as a salaryman at a major Tokyo company seems to strike at the core of his manhood. Rather, the circumscribed image of Ryōta's patriarchal figure is unbound by desire that flows beyond the strictures that give shape to the official boundaries of family in *Like Father, Like Son*. When Ryōta realizes that the son he has been raising is not his biological offspring, this knowledge challenges the boundedness of his domestic unit and his autonomy as a patriarchal figure. To remedy this problem, the Nonomiyas and Saikis initially choose to trade the children back, acknowledging the importance of blood in determining familial limits. Yet while the families submit to the demands of tradition, Ryōta's bonding with Keita emerges as a redundancy in the logic determining official designations of family, extending the bounds of their relationship beyond the limits it imposes. His love for a son that is not of his blood supersedes the rigid organizational strictures that give Ryōta authority, unbounding the corporeal form of both his person and his family by opening networks of interconnection that extend the designated borders of these units.

The framing of Ryōta's body at the end of the film reflects his change from an autonomous figure to an interconnected part of a larger collective, a space he shares with other bodies. Early in the film, medium shots isolate Ryōta prominently in the frame. However, toward the end, wide shots and sequences when the camera tracks his movement demonstrate the transformation of Ryōta's static body, characterized early on by permanence and stability, into one manifesting shifting interdependence. When Ryōta returns to the Saikis to search for Keita, his son flees from him, fearing that Ryōta has come to bring him back to his previous life. Accustomed to having others position themselves around his stationary form, Ryōta in this scene must chase after the boy. Captured in a wide shot that dwarfs him against the suburban backdrop, Ryōta becomes another body traveling through the space as he follows Keita down a covered shopping street. Not in control of where they go, Ryōta is tracked by lateral camera movement as he follows Keita along a path that runs parallel to the one on which Keita moves, while shot / reverse shots between the two reveal that Ryōta's path is on a lower level than the one on which his son walks, upsetting the hierarchy between the two. The desire that compels Ryōta to wander beyond the geographical boundaries of his authority (i.e., the corporate culture of downtown Tokyo) reflects his movement away from the source of his patriarchal influence: the hereditary-based institution of the nuclear family. This desire transforms his sovereign body into one manifesting change and dependence. The transformation of Ryōta's body is solidified in the final shot of the film, in which the Saikis and the Nonomiyas stand outside

Figure 10. Ryōta follows Keita through a shopping area in *Like Father, Like Son*.

the Saikis' home in one large group. Though not verbalized through dialogue, the blocking and body language of the characters seem to ask, "What do we do now? Who belongs to my family, and who belongs to yours?" Although no answers are provided, the lack of division in this congregation imagines the family not as a sovereign unit based in blood and lineage but rather as an open and evolving collective composed of actors with shifting identities and roles.

Figure 11. The Nonomiyas and Saikis pose separately in *Like Father, Like Son.*

Figure 12. The Nonomiyas and Saikis become one unit at the end of *Like Father, Like Son.*

A desire for truth that exceeds the limits dictated by the conventions of the courtroom drama in *The Third Murder* dislocates the bounded body of the lawyer-protagonist from its source of authority, resulting in new images of male corporality. The film represents a first for Kore-eda's career in more ways than one. It was his first film to be shot digitally in anamorphic widescreen and his first offering in the legal thriller genre (Konno and Kore-eda 98). Inspired by Hollywood courtroom dramas (Higuchi, "Kore-eda" 30), Kore-eda prepared for the film by attending the trials of several members of Aum Supreme Truth, an apocalyptic religious group responsible for a gas attack in March 1995 in the Tokyo subway system that killed several passengers and injured many more (Fukuyama and Kore-eda 23).[19] While the film rehearses some of the well-worn conventions of the courtroom genre, *The Third Murder* is driven more by Kore-eda's interest in capturing the nuances and complexities of the human experience rather than in meeting genre expectations. The film tells of the relationship between Misumi Takashi, a drifter accused of killing his former boss, and Shigemori Tomoaki, the lawyer tasked with defending him.[20] Despite overwhelming evidence indicating Misumi's guilt, Shigemori's push to uncover the truth behind his client's motive exceeds the function of a judicial system that is tasked with determining external notions of guilt within a legal context. Shigemori's interest in Misumi's case works to reveal the illusory nature of the phallic centrality that imbues his position in society with autonomy and symbolic influence.

Contrasts in the way the events of the film are narrated reveal the privileging of a traditional patriarchal perspective over a marginalized one. Patriarchal authority, as the film reminds us, is about not just the domination of men over women but also the influence that male figures at the center of power wield over men on the margins of society. The control exercised by the patriarchy over marginalized figures is thematized in the legal thriller, which involves powerful lawyers authoring a defense for their clients, often criminals with very little social capital. Much like the institutions of the family and the corporation, the legal system serves to center traditional notions of masculinity, representing the symbolic influence of the phallus. Initially, the divide between Shigemori and Misumi in terms of social status and access to the legal system is immense. With an impressive pedigree as the son of a former judge, Shigemori enjoys a level of socioeconomic prestige and influence as a lawyer. Raised in a broken home, on the other hand, Misumi is a convicted murderer—a crime for which he served thirty years in prison. In a strange coincidence, Shigemori's father tried Misumi's murder case—the first of the three murders referenced in the title of the film. The third murder most likely refers to Misumi's execution (which occurs off-screen) for the killing of his boss—the second murder. Misumi's guilt in the second murder is not open for debate. In the opening scene, we clearly see him bludgeon his boss to death and burn his body. Because this scene lacks stylistic embellishment and is shot using medium and wide shots in an objective and straightforward manner, the scene is framed in a way to suggest that it is not someone's version of events. The evidence that Misumi's defense team assembles appears to corroborate this account, which Misumi himself confirms.

By showing the murder in an unambiguous way, the film indicates that its focus is not on exonerating Misumi in the eyes of the legal system and the audience. He is clearly guilty according to the definition of culpability prescribed by the law. Instead, the film aims to depict Misumi's case in a way that challenges the basis of Shigemori's authority and masculinity. As the author of Misumi's case, Shigemori and his fellow lawyers have considerable power over him at first. They organize evidence into a narrative that serves to expedite legal proceedings, appropriating Misumi into a story decided in advance. In studying the Japanese legal system in preparation for the film, Kore-eda was surprised by the way that lawyers and judges often depend on "ready-made" narratives to frame cases (Ehrlich 139). All that is left to decide once the framework has been set is if Misumi's crime constitutes homicide or robbery homicide. However, Misumi's account of the murder is not bound by the same goals of the legal system or the narrative conventions of the genre, thus allowing his story to draw out other aspects of the crime.

In its attention to criminal psychology, the film references Japanese writer Shiga Naoya's short story "Han no hanzai" (Han's crime, 1913), from the I-novel (*shishōsetsu*) tradition of confessional writing. The story tells of a Chinese man, Han, and his unnamed wife who together perform a knife-throwing act in a circus. Han throws the sharp projectiles at his wife, who acts as a human target. One day, during their act, a knife thrown by Han strikes and kills his wife. As with *The Third Murder*, the event happens first in the story. Since the killing was performed in front of an audience, there is no doubt about what occurred, so the balance of the story becomes about whether Han meant to murder his wife and what really constitutes murder. The truth behind Han's intent, as the story suggests, is impossible to recover through the legal discourse that the lawyers bring to bear on the case; instead, the truth is located within Han's inner world. Consequently, the balance of the story involves Han working through his own thoughts to get to the truth of his actions. Similarly, because Misumi's role in the murder is shown at the start of the film, the balance of *The Third Murder* becomes more about the reasoning behind the murders. This motive comes to light when Misumi retracts his guilty plea later in the film, an act that reveals his multifaceted reason for committing the killing in the first place. Hired by his boss's wife to carry out the deed, Misumi was motivated partially by money but also to protect his boss's daughter, Sakie, who we learn was being sexually abused by her father. His retraction, as is implied in the film, is a way to shield Sakie, whom he befriends, from having to describe in open court the abuse she experienced. The lack of closure at the end of the film—Misumi's fate is only implied—was a way for Kore-eda to create a sense of uncertainty in a genre that usually ends with clarity, displacing the expectations associated with the legal thriller from the center of the story.

Narrative developments in the film initiate Shigemori's decentering from phallic centrality as well. Shigemori's interest in Misumi's motive pushes the story beyond the bounds established by the expediency of the legal system (and the expectations of the courtroom genre), displacing him from the narrative system that provides the foundation of his bounded subjectivity. Shigemori's interactions with Misumi bring about an identity crisis for the lawyer (Fukuyama and Kore-eda 25). The foundation of his authority—his legacy within the legal system that he inherited from his father, a foil to Misumi—falls apart, as he is unable to abide his father's outdated ideas. Shigemori's interest in Misumi as more than just a set piece in a premade narrative displaces Shigemori from his position as the author of Misumi's case. He is absorbed in Misumi's accounting of events, appearing as a character in the visual reenactment of the crime. He is also pulled into a fantasy sequence involving Misumi and his daughter—a scene in the film that does not work to determine

Misumi's guilt or innocence but sheds light on his motives for defending Sakie. In the scene, Shigemori reads a postcard written by Misumi to Shigemori's father after being released from jail for his first murder conviction. The postcard describes Misumi's memory of celebrating his daughter's birthday. Shigemori's visualization of Misumi's story draws upon the resources of television dramas to depict Misumi, his daughter, and Shigemori frolicking in the snow against the white backdrop of a Hokkaido landscape. The high-key lighting of this fantasy contrasts with the darker tones of the film to set the moment apart as a separate story from the rest of the narrative—a story in which Shigemori ceases to function as an appendage of the legal system from which he gained his authority.

The reworking of Shigemori's authority and identity is revealed through a shift in the way the film represents his corporal presence. Popularized by film critic Laura Mulvey's oft-cited 1975 essay "Visual Pleasure and Narrative Cinema," the *male gaze* refers to the way bodies, usually female, are treated in media as passive objects of erotic spectacle by male viewers. With its phallic centrality, the male body is often considered the possessor of the gaze and the subject of fantasies that objectify female bodies. Socially marginalized, Misumi transforms into a passive object of Shigemori's visual control in his jail cell and the camera's field of vision. In a three-shot like the one used to frame Ryōta and his family in the opening of *Like Father, Like Son*, Misumi speaks with Shigemori and the other lawyers in an interview room divided by a plate-glass window, which confines Misumi, leaving him powerless to escape. Shigemori and his fellow lawyers sit in a row as they question Misumi through the glass. In a scene that critics compare to one from Kurosawa Akira's *High and Low*, low-key lighting lends harshness to the interview room, suggesting a division between the two sides, while the scene's blocking and editing underscore the control that Shigemori and his team exercise over Misumi through the legal gaze. Shot / reverse shots of the bodies of the men on both sides of the glass juxtapose the authority of the lawyers with Misumi's marginalization as a passive object of their narrative and visual control. Misumi's solitary figure, dressed in casual clothing, contrasts with the authoritative image of the lawyers in dark business attire, who form a single, static body gazing back at Misumi, manifesting the advantage that they exercise over him.

While initially upholding a traditional power dynamic between the legal system and the criminal through the male gaze, *The Third Murder* exposes the illusion of the autonomy of Shigemori's masculine body vis-à-vis Misumi's subjugated form. Silverman questions the binary relationship implied in the idea of the male gaze between unified and authoritative male subjects and a powerless object of their visual scrutiny. The male gaze, for Silverman, does not affirm a plus value of authoritative presence but merely offsets the illusory nature of the subject's own claim to sovereignty. Performative in nature, the male gaze, Silverman suggests, provides a way for the subject to renew its connection to the phallic order by allowing it to project powerlessness onto the object of its surveillance (127). *The Third Murder* reveals the illusory nature of the patriarchal subject's claim to autonomy through merging the bodies that constitute both the subject and the object of the gaze. Initially separating Misumi and Shigemori on opposite sides of a sheet of glass, the cinematography and editing in scenes shot in the interview room obfuscate the power dynamic between the two characters; the interview room becomes a space in which the boundaries between the bodies of Shigemori and Misumi, as well as the actors who play these roles, dissolve. Though the original screenplay called for much of the film to take place in the courtroom, Kore-eda decided to add more scenes in the interview room after being impressed by the chemistry between Fukuyama and veteran actor Yakusho Kōji, who play Shigemori and Misumi, respectively (Fukuyama and Kore-eda 23). To capture the fluidity of their relationship, Kore-eda and his staff experimented with different camera angles to get the blocking of the characters just right (25). Though their early interactions are captured through shots that place each actor on opposite sides of the glass, in later scenes, conversations between the two are visualized from a lateral position, with the two men face-to-face. Shot at an angle that makes it appear as if there is no barrier separating the men, Shigemori begins to mirror Misumi's actions, suggesting his loss of power in the relationship. At one particularly tense moment, the camera breaks the 180-degree rule to temporarily reverse the position of the two men in the frame. Normally situating Shigemori on the right side and Misumi on the left, the scene cuts to a close-up shot of the two men's faces, this time with Shigemori on the left and Misumi on the right. Because their faces are obscured somewhat by shadows, for a moment we confuse their two bodies. The disorientation experienced through this break in visual continuity reflects the fluidity of the power dynamic between the two characters. The fluidity is also reflected in the dialogue, as Shigemori, who questions Misumi at the start of the scene, finds himself, by the end, being interrogated by the prisoner.

The emptiness of the traditional male subject is exposed in other Kore-eda films through acts of fetishization that lay bare each subject's own powerlessness. *Shoplifters* places men in conventional male roles as voyeurs of the female body only to expose the lack of anonymity that this posture seeks to conceal. The most salient example of voyeurism in the film occurs at Aki's sex club, where she performs a provocative

Figure 13. The camera jumps the 180-degree line in this sequence in *The Third Murder*.

Figure 14. The camera jumps the 180-degree line in this sequence in *The Third Murder*.

dance for a customer known only as Number Four, who watches on the other side of a one-way mirror. The first time Aki performs for Number Four, he remains anonymous behind the mirror—he sees without being seen. Shot from behind Aki, the scene allows us to see what he sees in the mirror: Aki's body as she performs for him. Subsequent scenes in the club, however, demonstrate that the whole setup is more than just a one-sided fantasy of a male subject—it is also the manifestation of that subject's own marginalization. Number Four reveals his powerlessness by projecting his castration onto Aki through fetishization. The men who sit on the other side of the mirrors are required to identify themselves as either a "breast" or "butt" man. According to Silverman, fetishization, which implies the obsessive focus on a particular body part, provides a means for male subjects to project their own incompleteness onto the object of their gaze through acts of visually dismembering body parts from the larger whole (127). Number Four's lack of anonymous influence, intimated through this fetishization of Aki's body, is exposed when Aki addresses him through the mirror, inviting him to a private talk room in which she can clearly see his face. The camera pulls in close to the mirror before which Aki dances to reveal the face of a man, concealed by a baseball cap, on the other side. The reflection of Aki's face in the mirror makes it appear as if she is sitting next to him. The powerlessness

Figure 15. Number Four's anonymous fetishization of Aki's body is laid bare in *Shoplifters*.

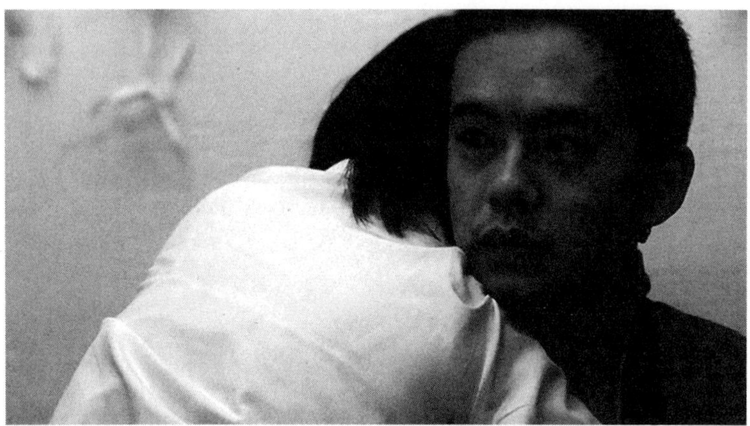

Figure 16. Number Four's anonymous
fetishization of Aki's body is
laid bare in *Shoplifters*.

that is hinted at through this exchange is fully revealed when the two meet in the talk room and are finally able to see each other face-to-face. As Aki embraces Number Four, he struggles to articulate a response, revealing that he has a speech impediment—a physical representation in the film of his symbolic castration.

The ultimate fetishized object—a sex doll—becomes a mirror of male lack in Kore-eda's film *Air Doll*. Based on a manga series by Gōda Yoshiie, *Air Doll* focuses on the experiences of an inflatable sex toy named Nozomi that comes alive one day. Initially, Nozomi—which translates as "wish"—manifests as a passive object of male desire. The doll belongs to a man named Hideo, a lonely bachelor who dresses Nozomi as a French maid or nurse each night. As his object of obsession, however, Nozomi lays bare Hideo's own lack of status and power: he works as a lowly waiter at a family restaurant and complains to Nozomi about being underappreciated. Nozomi's interactions with other male characters reveal their deficiencies as well. Becoming part of the living world, she takes a job at a video rental store—a place known for providing a means to satisfy fetishes—helping a lonely male customer search for films featuring a female protagonist with a certain type of hairstyle and a bored police officer find a film featuring a corrupt cop. Though the film's narrative perspective is initially focalized in the male perspective of Hideo, the viewpoint shifts to that of Nozomi and others. The cinematography reflects this decentering of a male perspective, as cinematographer Lee's use of mobile takes constantly reframes his subjects, deconstructing a stable point of view in the film. Capturing Hideo and Nozomi in a two-shot on a park bench in a scene after Nozomi comes alive, the camera jumps the axis line to record Nozomi's reaction to Hideo's attempted kiss. The lack of the phallic centrality of these characters, moreover, is reflected in the lack of their physical phalluses in the film. In place of male sex organs, Nozomi's plastic vagina insert is featured as the main metonym for intercourse, as it is repeatedly washed by her and others throughout the film. In one scene, before Nozomi comes alive, Hideo squats in his bathroom, cleaning the plastic receptacle as if he is cleaning himself.

Returning to *The Third Murder*, blocking in the interview scenes reveals shifting power dynamics between Shigemori and Misumi, while the visual commingling of their bodies dispels the illusion of the wholeness of Shigemori's bounded self. Margrit Shildrick describes the transformation that occurs to bounded, autonomous bodies when they come into physical contact with a marginalized form like that of Misumi: "And where the body of the other is uncertain and resistant to the demands of normative expression . . . touch figures as a moment of real threat, a troubling of the subject's illusion of purity and self-sufficiency" (*Prosthetic* 119). Although a gesture toward touch is made early in the film when Misumi places his hand on the glass and invites Shigemori to do the same, Shigemori and Misumi never actually physically touch. Instead, the subversion of the illusion of bounded corporality is carried out in the visual overlapping of their bodies through reflection in a scene that directly references the end of Kurosawa's *High and Low*. As Shigemori gazes upon Misumi, his own lack of self-presence is reflected back on him. The angle from which the interaction between the two is captured through the glass creates a double exposure shot, as an image of Shigemori is superimposed onto a close-up of Misumi's face, making it appear as if the two men are sitting side by side. As Shigemori leans forward, the reflection of his face overlaps with that of Misumi, briefly lining up, creating an effect not unlike the scene in Alfred Hitchcock's *The Wrong Man* (1956) when Henry Fonda's face is superimposed onto that of the true perpetrator of the murder that

Figure 17. Misumi's and Shigemori's bodies appear to merge in this double exposure shot from *The Third Murder*.

Fonda's character is accused of committing. Here the merging of the two images in the interview scene creates one composite, seemingly blending the identities of the two men by merging their bodies in the same space. Dispelling the illusion of a bounded self, Shigemori loses his physical presence, becoming a reflection cast over another form. By subverting the circumscribed autonomy of the traditional male subject embodied in Shigemori, *The Third Murder* ultimately questions the self-evident foundations that have served to define masculinities and shape their physical corporality in film culture.

Along with highlighting the illusory nature of bounded masculinities, Kore-eda's films envision alternatives to the traditional concept of male selfhood through bodies that do not serve as appendages of the patriarchal order—bodies that defy traditional definitions of stability and functionality. The bodies of day laborers such as Osamu in *Shoplifters* move, work, and play like normal men, yet with their marginalized status in the managed society, day laborers manifest as "others" to the authoritative bodies of doctors, lawyers, and businessmen played by actors such as Fukuyama in Kore-eda's films. The day laborer, Tom Gill suggests, has traditionally been treated as "antithetical" to the salaryman in Japanese culture (146). Accordingly, they are not held to the same expectations as their salaryman counterparts, including the need to serve as the pillar of their respective domestic units. The transitory nature of day laborers calls to mind the traditional wanderer archetype in film and drama that contrasts with the upwardly mobile salaryman and the economic development he represents. The image of the wanderer is perhaps best epitomized in Tora-san, the itinerant salesman and protagonist of one of the longest-running film series in Japan, *It's Tough Being a Man* (*Otoko wa tsurai yo*), which lasted from 1969 to 1995. Unbound by loyalty to a company, laborers lack the position and authority that salarymen gain through their association to a group. Their lack of stature manifests through bodies that defy idealized images of maleness in terms of dress and appearance. Unaffiliated with a company and traditional family, Osamu's diminutive form in *Shoplifters* represents his lack of social position. His passive body is carried home by coworkers after being injured at work, and he appears nude several times in the film, as Nobuyo, not Osamu, is depicted as the more sexually aggressive partner in their relationship. In fact, Kore-eda once partially jested that he chose actor Rirī Furankī to play Osamu because of his "beautiful back" (Rirī and Kore-eda, "Erosu" 35).

Male bodies that exist in between larger national boundaries in Kore-eda's films provide a model of masculinity that is not based on a circumscribed sense of "Japaneseness." In *I Wanted to Be Japanese* (*Nihonjin ni naritakatta*, 1992), a documentary made for the TV series *Nonfix*, Kore-eda deconstructs the basis of masculine bodies rooted in a national tradition. The film focuses on the life of a man named Kinoshita Atsushi who is caught between two countries, South Korea and Japan. A Korean national by birth, Kinoshita was forced to fight for the Japanese army in the Philippines during the war. After the war, he married a Japanese woman with the last name of Kinoshita. Taking her name as his own, he settled down to life in Japan. However, Kinoshita's true identity as a South Korean national named Park Yon-duk eventually comes to light, causing him to lose ownership of a hotel he ran in Japan and to be accused of espionage. After conducting interviews with those who knew Kinoshita in person, Kore-eda, with camera crew in tow, tracks him back to his hometown in South Korea but is unable to locate him. Fittingly, throughout the film, Kinoshita's physical form appears only in photographs. The lack of actual footage of him suggests that he transcends the bodily constraints foisted on national subjects, as he will forever exist in a space between two countries—one to which he belonged by birth and one in which he wished to live.

Bodies lacking normative functionality, moreover, manifest a corporality that comes about through interaction rather than as an expression of independent and autonomous utility. Kore-eda's interest in Sekine's story in *Without Memory* was certainly influenced by his own experience with the memory loss that he witnessed in his grandfather, who suffered from dementia when Kore-eda was young (Kore-eda, "Serote-pu" 373–74). In contrast to that of Kore-eda's grandfather, Sekine's memory loss resulted from medical malpractice: he was denied essential vitamins during his hospital stay due to cutbacks implemented by the government to reduce its health-care deficit, making beneficiaries responsible for their own care. Despite the attention the film places on the political implications of Sekine's case, Kore-eda's interest in his story is less about exposing a flawed health-care system and more about depicting the nature of a subject that is evaluated based on its ability to function as an independent and autonomous actor within the entrepreneurial health-care marketplace and the larger social sphere. The physical functionality that is often attributed to normative bodies—self-sufficiency in work and caring for oneself—is outsourced to a network of helpers in the film, providing a view of the male subject not as a fully functioning unit at the nexus of these operations but as one that gains meaning through its dependence on the functions outside of its own bodily forms. Lacking the capacity to operate independently in society, Sekine relies heavily on his wife and two sons, who collectively serve as a basis of continuity between past and present, something he is unable to do, as evident in a scene capturing an awkward shopping trip to the grocery store with one of his sons. Sekine utilizes other external resources to compensate for his lack of memory, including posted notes that serve as reminders and a journal in which he tracks his emotional reactions to daily events.

The bodies of men in Kore-eda's films, whether they are dependent, itinerant, or unbounded, reveal alternatives to the territorializing of the male body by the top-down forces of patriarchy and the national order. These men are formed by the demands of the phallic order, as well as by desire that transcends the logic and expectations of the family, the corporation, and other institutions that result from this order. As a result, masculine bodies move, work, and exist outside the parameters of the patriarchal order, figuring through networks that challenge the myth of the autonomy and the bounded nature of the masculine body.

Through these bodies, Kore-eda reworks identity, imagining the type of subject that emerges as Japan shifts away from the archetype of the feudal father and his family, roles that provided stability to the nation during its economic development after the war.

Body Moving: The Dynamics of Placemaking in *Our Little Sister, Still Walking,* and *After the Storm*

The worlds that Kore-eda envisions in his films are places of movement. Trains rush across the countryside, bicycles cruise down dark city streets, and bodies climb steep hills overlooking the ocean. This movement is directed by the larger socioeconomic forces that shape and define the urban settings of his films. The coding of territories formed under capitalism, argues Thomas Nail, designates a place for every element in these spaces, including the bodies that move through them (28). Yet if Kore-eda's films represent the ways these regulated places shape bodies and direct their movement, they also depict the way space is reimagined through the very passage of bodies through it, the way it is reconfigured through the dynamic interaction of travel captured on film. Even though the social and economic ordering of cities designates specific functions for organized spaces, film can capture how bodies temporarily remake these spaces through idiosyncratic movement that exceeds the spaces' function. Ultimately, this section argues, bodies in Kore-eda's films, the spaces through which they move, and the spectators who watch them form an assemblage that develops beyond the boundaries imposed by the demarcations of urban space and the cinematic form.

The demarcation of space, Kore-eda suggests, is of primary importance in the filmmaking process (Binoche and Kore-eda 167). Locations depicted in his visual narratives are not only authentic and real but also spaces formed through imagination. These two aspects of location—the actual and the virtual—continually collapse into each other in all forms of cinematic representation (Deleuze 68–97). Kore-eda melds the actual and the virtual in the representation of space by mixing documentary and feature film stylistics. Shooting all his films on location, Kore-eda faithfully captures life in the city streets and neighborhoods of Tokyo, Fukuoka, Hokkaido, and even cosmopolitan areas outside Japan, such as Paris and Seoul. The painstaking steps he takes to accurately depict real-world locations allow his films to make use of the virtual dimensions of filmmaking, imbuing these spaces with meaning. Setting *After the Storm* in the same Tokyo apartment complex in which he was raised, for instance, allowed Kore-eda to draw on his own experience in the process of imagining the film's fictional story.

The interrelationship between the virtual and the actual in the cinematic mediation of space is thematized in *After Life*. The process of shooting the memories of the visitors at the way station re-creates real locations through virtual sets while transforming virtual sets into authentic sites for new memories to take place. The emotional experience of remembering is triggered through both imagination and attention to verisimilitude. Striving for realism, the caseworkers research the details of Cessna airplanes and Tokyo streetcars, acquiring historically accurate props to aid in the re-creation of the past. When it comes time to shoot the memories, however, they rely on the resources of cinematic production to stimulate the sensory memory of the visitors, who stand aside, watching the production of their short films as codirectors. Crew members string cotton balls around the Cessna to replicate the feeling of flying through clouds and push the streetcar back and forth to reproduce the sensation of traveling through the streets on tracks. Through this layering of real and artificial elements within the mise-en-scène, *After Life* provides a metacinematic preview of the treatment of space in Kore-eda's subsequent films.

The intermingling of the real and the virtual represents both the limitations and the limitless possibilities of childhood in later films; it renders space both as a real location through a close attention to capturing the nuances of real-world sites and as an abstract space extracted through cinematography and editing that liberate the space from anchors to the real world. The Tokyo apartment and neighborhood that serve as the setting for *Nobody Knows* are figured both as actual places and as worlds of imagination where the children's zeal exceeds the harsh reality imposed by socioeconomic and geographical limitations. After hiding his siblings in the small apartment for several months to keep them from being discovered, Akira lets them loose into the streets one day. The use of handheld camera and rapid editing relays the children's joy in finally being able to leave their apartment. Filmed like a home movie, the scene is captured with tracking shots of the children running through the pathways surrounding their home, ignoring traffic laws, while a camera positioned close to the ground follows their feet as they dash through shopping centers and fool around at the local playground.

Similar to the plot of *Nobody Knows*, *I Wish* portrays the coming-of-age experience as one filled with hope and potential while also being determined by the reality of unavoidable social and familial circumstances. At the center of the film is a real-world event: the opening of a bullet train line between the Kyushu cities of Fukuoka and Kagoshima in 2011, the same year the film was released. To commemorate the opening of the line, Japan Railways Group asked Kore-eda to write a screenplay with a train theme (Takazaki and Kore-eda 70). From its inception, the bullet train has existed within the nexus of the real and the virtual in the Japanese cultural imagination, figuring both as a manifestation of the superiority of the national infrastructure and as a signifier of the limitless possibilities of its technological vision. Based on the actual expansion of the bullet train line, *I Wish* was filmed on and around train lines throughout Kyushu, instilling a sense of authenticity to the spaces portrayed in the film through a documentary style that captures real-world locations filled with authentic people, including the many nonactors who staff the stations the children visit along their journey (Kishida and Kore-eda 150–51). The authenticity of the setting creates a backdrop against which the characters' fascination for the bullet trains can develop. The limitless potential of high-speed rail travel captivates Kōichi's family. His grandfather, a semiretired confectioner, creates a new rice cake in honor of the event, and the children witness the magic of train travel everywhere; on their way home from school one day, they see an old lady on the other side of the tracks disappear before their eyes when a train zooms past in between them. Unlike the slow-moving commuter trains that transport the children on their journey, the bullet trains they watch (but never actually get to ride) embody the film's attempt to couch the wonder and potential of childhood within the unremarkable mundaneness of daily life. Shown at full speed as they race down the tracks, the bullet trains unleash a massive amount of energy that shakes the fence to which the children cling as they shout their wishes but nevertheless does not change the children's fate (indeed, Kōichi's family does not get back together). As the trains pass, a montage that strings together a series of images from the diegetic world, as well as those from the world outside the film, renders the locations in *I Wish* as both real places where everyday people live and visionary spaces in which anything is possible through the magic of filmmaking. Images of things the boys experience on the trip—a rice cake made by their grandfather and the hands of a station master—are mixed with shots of images from the world outside the film, including a series of photos of the two actors when they were younger and shots of wooden plaques

Figure 18. The mochi cake in the montage of scenes from the children's journey in *I Wish*.

Figure 19. A shot of the plaques left by the side of the train tracks in *I Wish*.

hanging near the bullet train lines on which the wishes of people who came to commemorate the passing of the trains in real life are recorded.

The blending of the actual and the virtual in the formation of the cinematic environments of Kore-eda's films affects the ways in which embodied subjects interact with them. Individual and collective bodies are shaped by the socioeconomic limitations that give form to the spaces that surround them. Brenner and Theodore argue that the "relentless drive to mobilize particular territories" in neoliberal systems continually transforms geographical areas, fashioning new locational grids (8). Characters in Kore-eda's films are determined by these forces. Scholars point to the constitutive nature of placemaking and its role in shaping subjects who exist within its boundaries. Deleuze and Guattari discuss the way the spaces of daily life are defined by the social and economic functions that are assigned to them: "The house is segmented according to its rooms' assigned purposes; streets, according to the order of the city; the factory, according to the nature of the work and operations performed in it" (*Thousand* 208). Accordingly, subjects are conditioned by a new set of limitations each time they move from one of these spaces to another: "As soon as we finish one proceeding we begin another, forever proceduring or procedured, in the family, in school, in the army, on the job. School tells us, 'You're not at home anymore'; the army tells us, 'You're not in school anymore'" (209).

Acknowledging the formative effects of placemaking on the subjects who exist within demarcated boundaries, Kore-eda depicts the transformation of bodies in his films within the larger social and natural environments in which they live. Places that are shaped by economic and social expediency in Kore-eda's films determine the formation of the communal bodies that reside therein. Financial trouble for a family-run café in *Our Little Sister* upends the routines of the main characters, who find community there. A regimented *danchi* in *After the Storm* gives shape to the flow of matriarch Shinoda Yoshiko's life and her relationship with her family members, a theme that is relayed by the tightly framed two-shots of Yoshiko and her daughter chatting side by side in Yoshiko's tiny apartment. In *Shoplifters* Yuri's small body is transformed within the space of the Shibata family house: she is given a haircut to conceal her identity and ointment to heal the bruises on her body that result from prior abuse.[21]

Physical movement through controlled spaces, moreover, integrates subjects into social, corporate, and familial organizations. Routes created by ordered cityscapes—public-transportation lines, streets, and walkways—move travelers around municipal areas in the direction and manner prescribed by the logic of urban planning as they assimilate into institutional collectives. Kore-eda often frames his compositions with telephone wires and other physical elements of urban organization to suggest the institutional structures that order the flow of bodies in his films. In an early montage in *Shoplifters*, Osamu is appropriated as an embodied subject of his social and corporate organizations as he travels through the city to the site of a construction job. Leaving the safe confines of his home, in which he has more autonomy, his body is immediately framed by the walls that surround his small street, appearing like a rat in a maze. Osamu's movement through his neighborhood is influenced by his role as a citizen with responsibility to his community. Carrying a bag of items to be recycled, he crosses the street to the designated recycling spot, following the lead of others whose paths to work are shaped by this civic duty. His socioeconomic status, moreover, is revealed when he is grouped with five other blue-collar workers in a van that will take them to the jobsite. The lack of individuation in this collective body is evident as one man holds a conversation on a cell phone while the others have no choice but to listen. In the next shot, Osamu's blue-collar body becomes one with his larger company through compulsory morning exercises. In the scene, all workers at the jobsite line up in well-ordered rows to perform morning calisthenics, a custom at Japanese workplaces. The unifying effect of the calisthenics on the workers' bodies is evident as they swing their arms in harmony as one large body. Finally, in an echo of the van scene, Osamu rides up a packed elevator at the construction site, surrounded by other workers, who crowd him in the tight frame. The regulation of the body by top-down influence reverberates in the next shot, in which Nobuyo is shown pressing clothes at a laundry facility along with a handful of other workers all dressed in the same uniform of the company for which they work.

Similarly, the grouping of subjects into socially defined domestic units is carried out through directed forms of movement. In *Maborosi* the widow Yumiko travels with her young son from Amagasaki, a city partway between the metropolitan areas of Osaka and Kobe, to a small

Figure 20. Osamu's body becomes one with his construction company in *Shoplifters*.

Figure 21. Osamu's body becomes one with his construction company in *Shoplifters*.

fishing village on the coast of the Japan Sea to join a widower to whom she is arranged to be married and his daughter. When the two families meet at the station, the camera unites the group in a wide shot, the silhouette of their bodies accentuating the formation of this new grouping. In *Like Father, Like Son*, moreover, the need to return biological children to their rightful parents initiates movement that solidifies the differences between two families of varying socioeconomic levels. The relocation of bodies in the film visualizes the rectifying of the mistake that led to the separation of these biological lines in the first place and a solidifying of a sense of collectivity sanctioned by the precedent placed on blood relations and social status as the defining aspects of family. The two families physically transform as they switch children partway through the film. Tracking shots that capture the Nonomiyas' black Lexus as it drives back and forth between their downtown apartment and the Saikis' home in the outskirts of Tokyo accentuate the way movement necessitated by social status alters the nature of bodily collectives. The repetition of similar shots on the trip to and from the Saikis' home—an image of Keita sitting in the back seat of the Lexus on the way there compares with one of Ryūsei sitting in the seat on the drive back—visualizes the reconstitution of these two families.

Yet if regulated spaces in Kore-eda's films give shape to bodies, directing their passage through demarcated zones and grouping them into collectives, the spaces themselves can be shaped by the bodies' very movement. In considering the way dynamic bodies in contemporary cityscapes have an effect on the terrain through which they pass, it is important to distinguish between the notion of *place* and *space*. In his much-cited study *The Practice of Everyday Life*, Michel de Certeau identifies places as ordered and stable grids that are delineated by urban planning and other systems of control; spaces, in contrast, are flexible and shifting fields that are constantly reorganized through use (117). Place is transformed into space, Certeau continues, by the movement of bodies through the "intersections of mobile elements actuated by the ensemble of movements deployed within them" (117). Thomas Nail likens the transformation of place into space to a game of leapfrog, in which the spatial demarcations of the game continue to change as characters jump over the bodies that form its physical boundaries:

[Places] set up some limits and by doing so create a new limit to cross, and so on itinerantly. Every time a territory is delimited, an outside or surplus is produced through this process of delimitation or "detachment." This surplus or credit is then redistributed to another line through an alliance, where it will again produce a surplus and so on in a perpetual disequilibrium, making its very dysfunction an essential element of its ability to function. In the territorial assemblage, the concrete elements become privileged and primary. Change happens progressively, one concrete point at a time. (30)

Places that direct movement through regimented zones transform in Kore-eda's films through the movement of bodies mediated by the virtual capacities of cinema. Counterbalancing the directed passage of Osamu through the city streets in *Shoplifters*, unproductive forms of movement also appear in Kore-eda's films, suggesting the possibility of movement that exceeds the functional logic of place. As a metaphor of this type of movement, the Ferris wheel that Kōichi rides with his grandfather in *I Wish* rotates in a trajectory that has no constructive function within the bustling city of Kagoshima. Movement like this that exceeds the utilitarian purposes of urban areas, moreover, works to redefine the functional potential of the space itself for the viewer. Certeau suggests that bodies that are not irrevocably tied to a role dictated by the places through which they pass reimagine the possibilities of this space through movement that surpasses the purpose of its original organizational design (70). Yet because travel is transitory in nature, travelers do not claim these places indefinitely, permanently redefining their purpose. Instead, they only borrow them temporarily, the visualization of which is made possible through Kore-eda's attention to the idiosyncrasies of movement in his films.

Characters in Kore-eda's films take ownership of public places, but only temporarily. During a typhoon in *After the Storm*, Ryōta and his estranged wife and son stake a claim in a public park, where they briefly reunite—but only for a few hours. By the next morning, the park has become a public place again. As liminal spaces that link one location to another, staircases provide a temporary stage that characters can personalize for their own use. Children playing on a public staircase used by commuters to get to the local station imagine a new purpose for this walkway in *Nobody Knows*. In *Still Walking*, the repeated use of a staircase that leads to the Yokoyama family home in the hills of the seaside Yokosuka area exceeds the official function of this walkway: to link the coastal area with the hillside homes. The Yokoyamas claim the walkway during the course of the day, transforming this public passageway into a private space each time the camera captures them ascending and descending it. The first time the stairs appear in the film, they are shot as a public place that directs the passage of community members up and down in regulated fashion. As Kyōhei ambles down the staircase on his morning walk to the beach, a runner passes him on his right, sharing the space with him. This same staircase, however, takes on an increasingly private function the next time it is shown, when Ryōta climbs with Yukari and Atsushi on their way to the Yokoyama house. As a high-angle shot looking down on the stairs captures them struggling with their luggage, the space becomes their own: they use it in a way that momentarily expands its narrowly defined function within the urban area. All alone on the staircase, Ryōta and his family pause for him to check his texts and to chat with Yukari about work and family, while Atsushi plays in the trees that line the staircase on either side. At the end of the film, Ryōta and Atsushi accompany Kyōhei on his morning walk to the beach, descending the stairs in a leisurely fashion. Ryōta stops to check his texts again, while Atsushi walks ahead, playing with the brush as before. By now, the staircase has become an essential part of defining their relationships as a family. The final time we see the staircase it is shot front-on as Kyōhei and Toshiko slowly ascend the stairs after seeing Ryōta and his family off at the bus stop. In this way, the repeated capturing of the characters' use of the space in a manner

Figure 22. Public staircases become personal places for characters in *Still Walking*.

Figure 23. Public staircases become personal places for characters in *Nobody Knows*.

that exceeds its official function temporarily transforms it from a place structured by city planning into a cinematic space made available as the setting for family bonding and a stage on which we see the passing of time.

Yet it is not just images of moving bodies but also the memory of these bodies that colors places in Kore-eda's films. The juxtaposition of the physical presence and absence of traveling bodies in *Maborosi* reframes the space in the viewer's mind through editing that directs attention to the emotional residue created by this passage. Early in the film, Ikuo rides his bike home at night through the dark city streets of his hometown near Osaka. The scene is captured primarily with minimal lighting and stationary cameras positioned along his route at a distance to track his path home. As Ikuo passes through the frame in various locations, shots often linger on the empty parts of the city through which Ikuo moves without cutting immediately to follow his progress. At one intersection, a camera placed at the end of the street captures Ikuo stopping, turning around, and going back the other way, following an idiosyncratic trajectory that defies the standard way of passing through the city and results in his late arrival at home. That the camera chooses not to keep his physical body in the frame for a few seconds after he moves through it emphasizes the impact of his passage through the space. This penchant for shots that linger on empty parts of the city—a technique that was criticized early in Kore-eda's career as excessive to the efficiency of visual storytelling—allows the director to focus the viewer's attention on the way space is transformed as characters move through it. Later, after Ikuo unexpectedly passes away, Yumiko cruises through these same parts of the city on her bicycle. As long shots capture her movement through the frame, we are unsure if it is Yumiko or Ikuo we are watching, as Ikuo's presence seems to linger in the dark city streets.

Indeed, by concealing bodies in the frame, Kore-eda is able to accentuate the effect they have on our perception of the space. The experience of emotional resonance in scenes in which characters are concealed demonstrates the way affect circulates apart from the bodily forms that are usually recognized as the nexus of emotional experience, allowing for the transformation of urban locations from cold, impersonal sites of function into a repository of sentiment and memory (Brennan 1–4). The use of naturalistic lighting in *Maborosi* draws attention to the lingering impression of voice, as concealing the physical source of the sounds by shadows in the frame draws attention to their importance, corroborating the idea that sound is more important than image. Protracted conversations among characters dressed in dark tones in dimly lit rooms before light is introduced to reveal bodies lend intimacy to scenes. Kore-eda conceals his characters within backgrounds to draw attention to the atmosphere that the bodies leave behind even as they are hidden within the frame. Yumiko's physical form, often covered in a long, dark dress, is obscured by shadows as she waits in a covered bus stop or sways back and forth on a train that is cast into darkness when it enters a tunnel. A scene at the end of the film in which she converses with her husband next to a funeral pyre is captured with a wide-angle lens that depicts their bodies as silhouettes on the vast shoreline while their voices are clearly heard. The fact that they only appear as silhouettes only increases the impact of the scene, as Yumiko's pain spreads beyond her body to fill the frame and color the landscape.

In *August without Him*, moreover, Kore-eda processes the emotional experience of Hirata's passing by capturing images of spaces that remind the director of him. Opening during the August after Hirata's death in May 1994, the film flashes back to the months leading up to his hospitalization as the narrator describes the final days of his life in the past tense. Family interaction in the film occurs through the experience of visiting emotionally charged locations. When Hirata returns to his hometown, his first trip in several years, he does not visit his living mother but instead goes straight to his father's grave at a local cemetery, lighting incense and pouring water over the stone before briefly addressing him. Depicting people through absence becomes a motif in the film as Kore-eda memorializes Hirata through shots of the ocean. After captions on a black screen inform the viewer that Hirata passed away on May 29, 1994, a voice-over reading a passage from Hirata's last essay is overlaid on a montage of summer scenes—a man walking by a harbor, a boat floating by the shore, and people frolicking on the beach. Though Hirata is physically present in the scenes leading up to the ending, the images of his enervated body on a hospital bed do not relay his joy for life like these scenes of summer. It is the absence of his physical form in the final moments of the film that transforms him from a social subject defined by his role as an activist and AIDS victim into an experience that circulates within the spaces he used to inhabit.

The dynamics of cinematic spectatorship are central to the remaking of space through movement in Kore-eda's works. In the same way that the bodily structures of Kore-eda's films form a space shared by filmmakers, subjects, and actors, they also form networks with the corporeal experience of the audience. The visceral relationship between bodies and film creates connections between characters, cinematic space, and spectators that extend beyond national traditions. Space in film, argues Kaisa Hiltunen, is co-opted in a material embrace among the audience, the embodied characters, and the fictional worlds they inhabit. This material embrace is due to the "tactile" nature of film, a characteristic of cinematic representation that is often disregarded in critical studies (Schofield 44–45). Not only do the dynamic effects of cinematography induce physical movement in embodied spectators—by making them turn their heads to follow camera movement, for instance—but film can also stimulate spectators' senses by emphasizing the interaction among characters who focalize their experience in the film and the physicality of the diegetic world (Hiltunen).

The prevalence of sensory imagery in Kore-eda's works conflates the bodily experiences of the characters with those of the spectator, connecting both to the spaces in which characters live and move. To ground spectators in a particular time and place in his films, Kore-eda fixates on the aural texture of everyday experiences—the crunching of potato chips in *I Wish* or the scrapping of frozen flavored ice in *After the Storm*. Kore-eda describes the importance of sensory experience in the representation of everyday spaces:

> In *After Life* I interviewed many ordinary people, asking them what they would choose as their most important memory. Actually, a sound or a song was the most common response. They also mentioned scents and tastes. Those senses leave an even more intense impression than images do. Surely sound is closer to the human essence than images. That's not a pleasant thing for someone involved in the image business to hear, but it doesn't seem right to me to think of the two as divided like that. In *After Life*, the middle-aged guy who chose the city tram as his favorite memory recalls a wealth of experiences after he gets on the tram and listens to a tape of its sound. I think people recall images that are evoked by sounds, and recall sounds that are evoked by images. I'm fascinated by images, so that's what I make, but I don't make such a rigorous distinction between the two. (Gerow and Kore-eda)

Kore-eda's prolific use of handheld cameras accentuates the visceral interaction with the physicality of the cinematic space. As the characters in *Distance* travel down the unpaved roads that lead to the lake in which their family members perished, their jostling back and forth, captured by the camera positioned in the backseat of the SUV in which they ride, makes viewers feel as if they are in the car too. This image is mirrored in a scene at the end when the characters return to the train station the next morning in the back of a flatbed truck, with the wind blowing through their hair as they make their way down the road.[22]

The sensory experience of movement captured in Kore-eda's films activates an embrace between embodied perspectives and the cinematic space, transforming the experience of locations. Giuliana Bruno highlights the "haptic" aspects of film that build a connection between spectator and environment through touch rather than just sight (6). For Bruno, the haptic mode of cinematic spectatorship is based in embodiment and kinesthesis, the way viewers sense movement through space by means of the physical action of characters who focalize the viewers' experience on-screen (6, 17). Extending this logic, Bruno argues that because acts of embodied kinesthesis are the central way for spectators to experience the spatial environment of films, they play a role in the formation and understanding of space itself: "Emphasizing the cultural role of the haptic, it develops a theory that connects sense to place. Here, the haptic realm is shown to play a tangible, *tactical* role in our communicative 'sense' of spatiality and motility, thus shaping the texture of habitable space and, ultimately, mapping our ways of being in touch with the environment" (6).

Kore-eda's films demonstrate the role embodied kinesthesis plays in the formation of the texture of space. Movement through space allows characters to physically interact with the world around them, transmitting these sensory data to viewers. The more visceral the movement, accordingly, the more travel can activate the imagination of the spectator, who experiences city spaces in film not only as the effects of urban planning—networks of roads and buildings—but also as repositories of sensation and memory processed through the virtual prism of film. For this reason, Kore-eda's visual narratives are often set in high locations: the hills of a coastal city in *Still Walking*, a cramped apartment on the top floor of a sprawling *danchi* in *After the Storm*, and cliffs overlooking the ocean in *Our Little Sister*. The strain of climbing up steep stairs and paths that lead to these places is captured through high- and low-angle shots that stimulate the tactile memory and kinesthetic experience of embodied spectators. Confused where to go when they arrive in their father's remote hometown to attend his funeral, Chika and Yoshino in *Our Little Sister* are met at the train station by Suzu, who walks with them to the family inn in the hills. On the way there, Suzu decides to take a short cut that leads up a sharp incline through the woods. A high-angle shot captures the three sisters at the bottom of the slope, suggesting a daunting climb for the girls, especially Yoshino, the laziest of the three. Cutting to a low-angle shot of the sisters climbing the slope from behind, with Yoshino struggling in the back, accentuates the sensation of ascending the steep hill.

The strain of climbing is captured again later when Suzu takes her sisters to her favorite location in the town. A jump cut segues to a high-angle shot of the sisters climbing yet another hill, this time joined by the eldest sister, Sachi. Again, we see Yoshino struggle to ascend the path, huffing and puffing as the steep incline affects her gait. The shots of Yoshino's physical struggle against the terrain humanize her in the viewers' minds as the character to whom they can relate, and the sensory information relayed by her struggle serves to unite viewers in an embrace with the physical world of the film. We feel how steep the hill is through her complaints. Because embodied viewers are linked to the environment of the film through the mediation of the characters who move through it, the transmission of this experience colors the diegetic world, altering the function of the space in the viewers' eyes. The cinematic representation of character movement then transforms places captured on film from impersonal locations in the preestablished geography into spaces full of meaning for both characters and viewers.

Kore-eda imbues scenes of movement with both sentiment and sensory data, which further reinforces ties among characters, viewers, and space. Sentimental moments in Kore-eda's films frequently occur after scenes of strenuous walking, often to the high locations in which the films are set. Characters build ties with family by climbing up hills to visit the graves of loved ones in *Our Little Sister* and *Still Walking* and by taking long walks through the city in *Like Father, Like Son.* The emotional experiences shared by characters and spectators after strenuous movement to meaningful locations allow them to put their mark on the space, to make it their own. When the sisters reach Suzu's favorite place at the top of the steep hill, they are captured in a four-shot, staring out at the valley below, a site that reminds them of their hometown in Kamakura. As they look out at the valley, comparing it to their home, Sachi thanks Suzu for taking care of their father before he died. As Suzu begins to cry, Sachi embraces her sister, and the camera cuts to a four-shot behind the sisters, who stand gazing out at the view. The physical experience of climbing up the mountain, coupled with the sentiment that the characters and viewers share at the top, transforms the valley setting from an unknown space into one that is infused with meaning for both the characters and the viewer.

Later, when Suzu moves in with her sisters in Kamakura, the visceral and emotional experience of movement allows her to become a part of Kamakura and allows Kamakura to become a part of her as she walks on the beach, climbs hills overlooking the ocean, and rides her bicycle around town. Eager to show her his favorite spot in Kamakura (in the

Figure 24. Ascending hills relays the visceral experience of moving through space in *Our Little Sister*.

Figure 25. Ascending hills relays the visceral experience of moving through space in *Our Little Sister*.

same way Suzu introduced her sisters to her hometown), a young boy from Suzu's new class doubles her on his bike up a steep hill. The awkward scene relays the boy-meets-girl melodrama of the film's source material—a *shōjo manga* (popular comics created for young women)—filling viewers familiar with these comics with giddy expectations about a budding romance between the two. As the two reach the top of the hill, a high-angle tracking shot captures them quickly descending under a tunnel of blooming cherry trees that line both sides of the road. As the camera pulls in close to Suzu's face, a POV shot of the white blossoms falling from the trees above alternates with a close-up of Suzu's petal-covered face overlaid on the concrete streaming by below, highlighting the transformation of her body. As movement allows Suzu to become one with this new space, the sensation and emotion created by the visceral strain of the bicycle ride and the references to *shōjo manga* color the space for the viewer, making Kamakura our space too.

Though places become private spaces through character movement, Kore-eda's films remind us of the temporary nature of this process, the way the public and the private work in tandem to shape the settings through which characters move. *After the Storm* levels the divide between public and private space by depicting movement that is directed by the larger logic of the city and that exceeds this logic through more idiosyncratic forms of travel. Shaped by both the public and the private experience of space, characters in Kore-eda's films are often introduced on trains and buses, like the recently married Ryōta in *Still Walking* and the novelist Ryōta in *After the Storm*. Trains in these two films figure as both a symbol of mobility and a way of standardizing movement

Figure 26. Descending hills relays the visceral experience of moving through space in *Our Little Sister*.

within the city. Certeau points out the paradoxical immobility of train passengers riding on modes of transportation that take them through the city in rapid fashion: "The unchanging traveler is pigeonholed, numbered, and regulated in the grid of the railway car, which is a perfect actualization of the rational utopia" (111). *After the Storm* utilizes trains and other forms of public transportation to depict cinematic spaces as both private and public at the same time. At the start of the film, Ryōta travels by train and bus and on foot to get to his mother's apartment complex in the Nerima district of Tokyo. Captured in a sequence of shots linking locations throughout Tokyo, Ryōta is directed in a linear fashion through the city by these public-transportation systems. Yet his movement temporarily diverts from this prescribed path as he ambles through the train station, stopping along the way to eat noodles, enjoy a drink, and take part in other activities that exceed the function of the space and the development of the narrative while also relaying the sensory experiences of eating and drinking that allow viewers to relate to the visceral experience of moving through the space.

Certainly, characters in Kore-eda's films are at the mercy of the spaces that surround them: the sprawling streets, the extensive public-transportation system, large apartment complexes, and other manifestations of contemporary society organize family units and communities

Figure 27. Ryōta is introduced on a train in *After the Storm*.

and standardize the movement of bodies through these spaces. The mediation of cinematic techniques, however, allows Kore-eda to imagine a virtual view of space in his films to go along with the socioeconomic realities that it presents. As virtual images, accordingly, these transitory spaces have the potential to transform into something else, to take on new meaning as bodies pass through them. Movement that defies a prescribed manner of interacting with space, such as wandering and performing private functions in public spaces, highlights a potential role for spaces that defies their organizational function. The construction of space through excessive movement in Kore-eda's films underscores the way even the most regulated parts of urban cityscapes are given form through the physical interaction of the bodies that pass through them. While this form of movement is not subversive—it does not change the prevailing power structure but operates within it—it provides a new way of considering the interaction between bodies and urban areas captured on film.

Private and Public Bodies of Memory in *After Life*, *The Truth*, and *Distance*

This final section delves deeper into an issue about Kore-eda's films that has been discussed widely: memory. Building on the discussion of shared spaces of memory in the previous sections, this section argues that the function of memory in Kore-eda's works is more focused on the present than the past. In so doing, this section seeks to contextualize his films within a neoliberal worldview that effaces the past and eradicates historical awareness by "eterniz[ing] the current economic order" and "absorbing in itself both past and present" (Traverso). A consequence of the creating of a "perpetual present," critic Christian Cercel argues, is the disruption of communities built around shared ties to a common history (8). Kore-eda's films and documentaries—including *After Life*, *The Truth*, and *Distance*, among others—reveal the loss of the past within a neoliberal worldview and the effect of this loss on the formation of communities in the here and now. Disconnected from the past, the socialities depicted in films such as *Distance* regenerate around acts of remembering that underscore the fate of history in contemporary times while manifesting new possibilities for community building at a time when the collapse of distinctions between present and past erodes the potential for meaningful social action.

The treatment of memory in Kore-eda's films manifests as both a reflection of neoliberal influence and a response to the loss of community that neoliberalism induces. In one sense, both the process of memory and the worldview imagined through neoliberalism treat the past in the same way: they seek to efface a sense of history in the formation of an eternal now. Discussing the differences between these two modes of processing the past, Peter Novick suggests that history involves an ordering of the past as past and the present as present, whereas memory seeks to bring the past into the present: "Memory works selectively as part of the myth making needs of the group in the present. History is more about the historicity of events. The idea that they took place then and not now" (4). The contrast between history and memory that Novick identifies invites new possibilities for communal experience based on rituals that re-create the past in the present. The relative lack of flashbacks in Kore-eda's films, despite their thematic attention to remembering, indicates a view of memory that is more focused on the living present.[23] Indeed, acts of remembering in Kore-eda's films are the product of a collective experience in the here and now, the result of a moment in which the process of memory extends beyond the boundaries of an autonomous subject to form shared spaces around communal acts of commemoration.

Self-referential attention to the operations of filmmaking in *After Life* and *The Truth* reimagines the privatized process of remembering, drawing the focus away from subjects who retrieve information from their own past and redirecting it to a communal re-creation of the past in the present. Filmmaking is analogous to memory in Kore-eda's films. The process of recording and viewing cinematic images in general, argues Susannah Radstone, replicates the process of remembering itself (326). More than any other of Kore-eda's films, *After Life* and *The Truth* draw attention to the connection between memory and cinema through rituals of filmmaking performed in the present. The way station at which the deceased are greeted by caseworkers in *After Life* resembles the municipal offices found in all Japanese cities. The bureaucratic functions of daily life—applying for birth and death certificates, among other things—occur in these offices. As we learn later in the film, there are many way stations established to process the newly deceased, suggesting that citizens are assigned to a particular station based on where they live. Waiting to speak with caseworkers, visitors sit in a drab reception area befitting a government office building until they are summoned to an interview room. In these meetings, caseworkers probe visitors, seeking specific details about each individual's favorite experience in the past that will facilitate its re-creation on set. The gaps in the memories of the visitors, like the gaps in a screenplay, require staff and visitors to work together to reconstruct the past through the resources of filmic representation. In staging the memory of an elderly woman, Tamara Kimiko, at a dance hall in Tokyo after Japan's surrender during World War II, workers prompt Kimiko to remember the particulars of the experience. Doubting her own powers of recall, she does her best to fill in the details, drawing a rough sketch of the dress she wore to the hall and instructing the child actress who plays her in the film how to perform the dance. Holes in her memory require the staff to improvise on the fly as they re-create the experience on set. A handheld camera captures Kimiko rehearsing with the actors, positioning her in the role of a director in the production of her own memory. Participating in the cinematic re-creation of the past with others, moreover, gives rise to emotional connections with family that are more palatable than the illusive memories themselves. As Randall Halle suggests, experiences "color" memory, making it more vivid (684). The process of shooting an elderly woman's experience of making rice balls with her family in a grove of trees in the immediate aftermath of the devastating 1923 earthquake in Tokyo becomes the memory itself. Rehearsing the scene, the woman teaches the staff, who play the members of her family, how her family made rice balls when she was a child. Along with the preparations for shooting the actual scene, the time she spends with the workers imaginatively remaking the event channels the transcendent emotional experience of the memory itself.

The recasting of memory from a private function into a collaborative process transforms characters from socially formed subjects into an expression of communal filmmaking in the present. Watanabe Ichirō's wife, Kyōko, we learn, died a few years earlier, passing through the same station. Unbeknownst to Ichirō, Kyōko's ex-fiancé, Mochizuki Takashi, who died in World War II, is a caseworker at the station and is assigned to help Ichirō during his stay. Takashi has remained at the way station, we learn, because he was unable to decide on his own memory during his time as a visitor right after his death. Takashi helps Ichirō choose a memory by providing him the VHS cassettes on which he views his life.[24] Shot front on with a stationary camera, as discussed in a previous section, each scene captures Ichirō's life as a bureaucratic subject, a product of the top-down institutions to which he was beholden during his humdrum life. Struggling with indecision for much of his stay at the station, Ichirō eventually chooses a simple memory of sitting on a park bench with Kyōko in Tokyo's Hibiya Park. The remaking of this memory not only builds on the footage presented in the videotape but also exceeds its purely documentary function, becoming a product of the creative input of cast and crew, who share in the memory of creating it. Though we never actually see it in *After Life*, the scene is most likely shot on a sound stage, with actors who perform the roles of Ichirō and his wife. Watching his life processed through the imaginative filter of filmmaking allows Ichirō to reenvision the scenes of his life captured by the neutral objectivity of the video tapes, freeing him to experience the sentiment of the moment.[25] His transformation from a social subject documented on the VHS tapes into a result of cinematic production is evident in his disappearance from the theater when the houselights turn on at the end of the screening.

Not limited to Ichirō's imagination, however, this memory becomes a shared experience for Takashi, one that also bonds him with his fellow crew members at the way station. At the end of the film, Takashi finally chooses his own memory, but not one from his mortal existence. Sitting on the same bench that was built to shoot Ichirō's memory, Takashi acknowledges the space as a film set rather than as a re-creation of a Tokyo park. A shot / reverse shot sequence that breaks the fourth wall underscores the staged nature of the set. A long shot of Takashi looking off frame while sitting on the bench in the dark studio cuts to capture what he sees: his fellow crew members standing behind a camera against a backdrop painted to appear like heaven, with clouds covering a blue sky. Kore-eda suggests that the shared space of memory created through the collaborative filmmaking process is illustrated in the two intertwined rings on the iconic flag of the way station itself (Paletz and Saito 55).

Made over twenty years later, *The Truth* (2019) echoes *After Life*'s attention to the communal acts of remembering in the present,

Figure 28. *After Life* draws attention
to the process of film production.

Figure 29. *After Life* draws attention
to the process of film production.

thematizing the rewriting of memory in the space between the film set and the outside world. The screenplay for *The Truth* is based on an unpublished script that Kore-eda penned in the early 2000s titled "Kurōku" (Cloak), which sat for several years before he revised it in 2011 (Hori and Kore-eda 26). After searching for years for a project in which he could cast Binoche, a longtime fan of Kore-eda's work, Kore-eda experienced an epiphany on a plane ride back to Japan after a promotional tour for *Our Little Sister* in Paris. He realized that he could rewrite the script to allow Deneuve and Binoche to play the mother and daughter roles of Fabienne and Lumir (26). The tense relationship between Fabienne and Lumir comes to a head when Lumir and her small family return to Paris for a week to celebrate the release of Fabienne's memoirs, also titled *The Truth*, just as Fabienne begins shooting a new science fiction film, *Memories of My Mother*, a film within a film based on a short story by real-life author Ken Liu. *Memories of My Mother* tells of the relationship between an earthbound daughter and her absentee mother, who resides in outer space, where time does not flow at the same rate, in an effort to staunch the growth of her cancer. The mother returns to the earth every seven years to visit her husband and daughter. Bound to the earth, the daughter continues to grow throughout the story, while the mother remains the same age. The story of a daughter's struggle to relate to a mother who never ages certainly reflects Lumir's efforts to connect with her larger-than-life mother, a product of the persona that she assumes as a luminary in the French film world. The strained relationship between the two is aggravated by the content of Fabienne's memoirs and the rosy way it glosses over some of the difficult episodes in their past, depicting Fabienne as more of a maternal presence than Lumir remembers. However, Fabienne prefers poetry over the strictures of journalistic accuracy and repeatedly reminds her daughter not to trust memory.

In *The Truth* efforts to bridge the divide between the conflicting views of the past held by mother and daughter initiate shared acts of remembering in the present. Fabienne and Lumir collaborate in the construction of this shared space through acts of storytelling and performance that elicit truthful moments. Events occurring both in the film studio and in the world outside of the set blend moments of creative fabrication with genuine emotion. In an interview with Kore-eda,

Binoche commented on the way acting and storytelling can reveal a portion of truth, even though they are usually associated with fiction and lies (Arai 18). To further bridge the divide between the set and the outside world, Kore-eda based the characters in *The Truth* on the real-life experiences of Deneuve, who, like Fabienne, has won two César Awards (the highest honor in the French film industry), and Binoche, who, like Lumir, was raised by an actress (21). Fabienne is a star on and off the set. In scenes capturing her life outside of the studio, she is often shot head-on, positioned in the center of the frame as she rides in the backseat of her chauffeured car on the way to work or chats in interviews. Her face is always illuminated with soft lighting, even in scenes shot outdoors or in sunny locations. She saunters around her large Paris home, practicing her lines and making acerbic quips, while those who attend to her—her manager, boyfriend, and ex-husband, along with Lumir and her family—play the part of attentive audience members in the dramas she creates. Yet if the "real" world outside of the set manifests as a place of performance, the creative space of the studio prompts moments of genuine emotion and insight. The embedded film, *Memories of My Mother*, avoids a direct mirroring of the world outside the studio by reversing the roles that Fabienne and Lumir play onstage and in their private lives. But performing the part of a daughter of a woman who never seems to age allows Fabienne to understand her own daughter's experience being raised by a mother with transcendent fame. Likewise, Lumir sees her relationship with her mother anew as it is re-created onstage, as Fabienne's character is visibly more aged than the role played by her costar at the end of the film. As Fabienne draws on emotion from the relationship with her daughter to fuel her fictional performance on set, the impact of her performance heightens the emotional resonance of her daughter's memories.

This intertwining of fictional performance and authentic emotion allows for a collaborative rewriting of the past. Screenwriting and improvisation provide metaphors for shared acts of remembering. Lumir writes Fabienne's lines on and off the set, crafting email correspondence for her mother, working as her temporary manager, and revising her lines for the film. She relies on the memory of a fight with Fabienne to create authenticity in a scene in *Memories of My Mother* between the fictional mother and daughter, Fabienne and her costar. Fabienne and

Lumir argue over Fabienne's mistreatment of a family friend named Sarah, an old rival of Fabienne in the film world and a mother figure (until she died at a young age) for Lumir. Lumir's revising of her mother's lines reflects her process of rewriting a shared memory with her mother, allowing her to reframe the past. Fabienne, too, reframes the past, channeling it through her performance in the film. Truth becomes part of the fiction for her: Fabienne depends on memory to inspire her performance onstage and on the resources of acting to renew her perspective on her relationship with her daughter. As Lumir changes the script, Fabienne reacts through her acting. The director captures spontaneous moments of real emotion from Fabienne inspired by her experiences with her daughter. Fittingly, the harmonizing of private acts of remembering by Fabienne and Lumir occur within the boundaries of the set when the two pass on a dress owned by Sarah to Fabienne's costar, who serves as a proxy for Sarah. Putting on the dress, the costar assumes a role in the production of Fabienne's and Lumir's memories, allowing the two to remake the past and momentarily find a shared space within the discord that exists between their individual recollections of it.

Acts of remembering in the present through the film-within-a-film setups of *After Life* and *The Truth* provide a model for the communal

Figure 30. *The Truth* draws attention to the meta-aspects of film production.

forms of memory that Kore-eda depicts in subsequent family dramas, forms of remembering that extend beyond the boundaries of the memory function of individual characters. Acts of remembering depicted in Kore-eda's films conflate the experiences of the director and even audience members. Wada-Marciano suggests that remembering in Kore-eda's *Still Walking* manifests as a social act in which the memories of the characters are conflated with the audience ("Dialogue" 116). Through a process described as "confabulation," Kore-eda creates a "dialogue" between his recollection of his own family life, that of his characters, and even those of the viewers of the film through references that unify the memory of all three (116). Kore-eda wrote the screenplay for *Still Walking* right after the death of his own mother, when his recollections of her and their family life together were still fresh in his mind (Kanazawa and Kore-eda 50). Details from the film—the broken tiles that line the bathtub of the Yokoyama family home, for instance—are memories that Kore-eda carries from his own childhood (50).

In crafting the home life of families, moreover, Kore-eda seeks to relay personal experiences in ways audiences can understand, such as incorporating into *Still Walking* intertextual references to works of classical Japanese cinema with which they would be acquainted (Wada-Marciano, "Dialogue" 116–17). Kore-eda used this same technique in *After Life*, the original screenplay of which connected the memories of the visitors at the way station to major historical events that Japanese audiences would also remember, including the Kantō earthquake of 1923, the occupation of Japan after its defeat in World War II, the student radicalism of the 1960s and early 1970s, and the bubble economy of the 1980s (Ellis 35). At the same time, the conflation of memory in *Still Walking* and other films is not always a harmonizing experience for the characters. Kore-eda explores the ethical implications of shared acts of remembering that can serve a coercive end. In *Still Walking*, the matriarch of the Yokoyama family, Toshiko, tortures those who have angered her, using the past as a weapon with which she periodically beats offenders. She uses this weapon on Yoshio, the boy who cost her son his life when he died saving Yoshio from drowning. Every year, Toshiko invites Yoshio to visit the home and pay his respects to her son, refusing to let him forget his part in her son's death. Toshiko also tortures her husband, who cheated on her in the earlier years of their marriage, by repeatedly making the family listen to the song that she heard coming from the apartment of the woman with whom he was having an affair.[26]

The emphasis on recovering memory through rituals performed in the present in Kore-eda's films allows for the formation of communities built around the commemoration of the past. These commemorative communities are unique in that they do not give themselves over to the violence that often characterizes these types of groups. The creation of an eternal now in neoliberal culture, as reflected in Kore-eda's films, inhibits sociopolitical action by neutralizing the capacity for individuals and groups to locate a historical referent that gives meaning to political endeavors undertaken in the present (Traverso). In his analysis of *Distance*, Je Cheol Park argues that the film represents an attempt to "imagine a new community in response to the decline of a larger national one" amid the influences of globalization and neoliberalism (167). While the film certainly represents an attempt to realize a new sense of community, I suggest that *Distance* reimagines the relationship between the past and present, forming a sense of sociality among fellow mourners that re-creates the collective spirit of some of the social and political movements of Japan's recent past without echoing their call to revolution.

Distance follows the experiences of four protagonists whose family members were involved in a terrorist attack committed by a religious group known as the Arc of Truth. Arc of Truth members, we learn, released poison into the water supply of a Tokyo suburb and then committed mass suicide on the banks of a lake near their remote cabin hideout. The Arc of Truth recalls two violent groups from Japan's recent past that are conflated in the Japanese cultural memory of the 1990s and 2000s. The Aum gas attack in the Tokyo subway system captured the imagination of the Japanese public for much of the 1990s and early 2000s partly because this attack recalled another violent event that occurred two decades earlier, the United Red Army Incident of 1972. An insular faction of socialist revolutionaries that was formed toward the end of Japan's extremist era of the late 1960s and early 1970s, the United Red Army (URA) sought to prepare for worldwide revolution in the winter months of 1971–72 by holding a training camp at a remote cabin in the mountains of the Nagano prefecture. The draconian methods the group used to prepare its members for the psychological rigors of revolution resulted in the lynching of several URA members, whose bodies were found buried near the cabin. After authorities were alerted to its location, the group scattered in different directions. With police in pursuit, five URA members barricaded themselves in a lodge in the mountains surrounding the resort town of Karuizawa, holding the wife of the lodge's caretaker hostage as they repelled a force of three thousand riot police in a siege that lasted ten days and was broadcast live on public television. In the years following the subway attacks, Aum and the URA were linked by cultural sources that sought to process the events by representing Aum through the image of the URA and the URA through the image of Aum (Yamada 14).

The small community formed by the surviving relatives of those who died in the Arc of Truth incident in *Distance* evokes the sociality of the religious group itself without reproducing its violence. On the third anniversary of the incident, members of this community make their way to the lake where their relatives perished. The members include Kiyoka, a schoolteacher whose husband left home to join the Arc of Truth; Makoto, a middle-aged man abandoned by his believer wife; Masaru, a part-time swim coach mourning his buttoned-down older brother; and Atsushi, a young florist whose connection to the incident is unclear. They meet at a remote train station and drive together by SUV into the wooded area surrounding the lake. Parking by the side of the road, the group trudges through the dense forest before arriving at a narrow, wooden pier extending over the water. Walking to the end of the pier, they take turns memorializing their family members, dropping flowers into the water and offering silent prayers, after which they eat lunch in a clearing near the shore, engaging in casual conversation. When they return to their parking spot, however, they discover that their SUV is missing, presumably stolen or towed. It is getting dark, and they have no cell service. While debating what to do, they run into a former member of the Arc of Truth, a young man named Sakata, who is also at the lake to commemorate the anniversary of the deaths of his fellow members. Sakata, too, is stranded in the forest; his motorbike was removed as well. Without the means to return home, they decide to spend the night in a cabin near the lake—the same cabin used by the Arc of Truth members in the days leading up to their demise.

The members of the group both remember and forget their relatives by replicating and reliving their experiences. Like that of their predecessors, the relationship among members of this new community is based on social alienation. Members of the Arc of Truth sought to forge connections with others outside mainstream society, and the stigma of being associated with this religious group has bonded this new community together as a makeshift family. The characters are often framed together, walking through the forest, waiting at the train station, and dozing on the train. Protective of one another, they show concern when individuals venture off on their own into the dense forest or the dark night. Family sentiment is conveyed through the home-movie style that captures events in the film. Shot in the Nagano prefecture over the course of ten days, *Distance* came together through a largely extemporaneous mode of production (Shimamori and Kore-eda 167). The trip to the lake is captured primarily through a handheld camera positioned at human height, moving without smooth tracking, to make the experience personal. Jump cuts stitch scenes together often haphazardly, without the appearance of artistic design.

The familiarity created through this home-movie style allows a sense of the past to reside in the present. For this reason, the cabin serves less as a memory archive in which the visitors locate meaning buried there. Although Sakata was present in the days leading up to the incident at the cabin, he is unable to provide any insights into the thoughts and motivations of Arc of Truth members. Instead, the characters remember the past by replicating it in the present, reenacting the experiences of their family members. Forced to spend the night in the cold cabin, they huddle together like the Arc of Truth members on the eve of the attack, whiling away the hours together by trying to imagine what their loved ones experienced in the days leading up to the poisoning. An abstract past to which they lack access is given material form through their physical engagement with the hallowed space of the cabin: they walk on the same floors and sleep in the same rooms as those who came before. Their visceral engagement with the space shifts the epistemological weight of the Arc of Truth experience away from the past and places it on the actions performed by the group in the present, who form a new community through commemoration while sharing the past and the space with those who came before.

The ambivalence of this new community toward a past to which they have no access allows them to re-create the sociality of the Arc of Truth while forgetting the group's ideological legacy. The companionship they enjoy merely provides communal support rather than serving as a call to transform the world through violence. In contrast to the radical spirit of the Arc of Truth, the new community engages primarily in secular conversations. Flashbacks to moments that occurred before the poisoning reveal the characters' rejection of the esoteric beliefs their family members sought to share with them. When their overnight trip to the lake comes to an end, each member of this new community returns to their private life within the secular world that their family members rejected. The fact that the characters can create a community around the act of commemoration in the film suggests that meaningful connection and even social action inspired by the past are possible amid the eternal present, even if that action falls short of its revolutionary aims. In this way, *Distance* both acknowledges the continued need for communities in contemporary society formed around past collectives and seeks to quell the more toxic elements that emerge in their efforts to advocate for and even seek social change.

Although often described as a contemporary "memory director" (Paletz and Saito 52), Kore-eda seems to focus more on the process of forgetting than the act of remembering in his visual narratives. Even though the act of remembering is often associated with forming individual and communal identities, Kore-eda's films seem to place importance on actually living in the present and not in the past as a way of realizing it. The actual past is a static place with little energy, as the sequences from Ichirō's life in *After Life* demonstrate. Instead of relying on the past, characters absorb cultural and communal memory by simply existing in and experiencing the world, sharing it with those from their memories. Lacking long-held family traditions that could bind them together, the Shibatas unite around new rituals and activities. Similarly, even though canning plums at their grandmother's home is a long-held tradition based in memories that Suzu does not share with her three sisters in *Our Little Sister*, the act of canning itself becomes the most important part of uniting them as a family. By living in the present, characters not only gain identity but also integrate, or reintegrate, into society. Nozomi in *Air Doll* learns to be a human and a woman just by leaving her owner's apartment and engaging in the world outside, while the children in *Nobody Knows* discover how to be more like typical children when they spend time outside their apartment with other children their age.

Concluding Thoughts

Though it may be impossible to completely extricate Kore-eda's work from the interpretive context of Japanese film and culture, the response that his film poses to the values and experience of a neoliberal worldview extends the relevance of his work beyond the narrow confines of the bounded national tradition of Japan. At the heart of Kore-eda's films is an attempt to express the value, importance, and agency of human experience amid the larger economic, political, and social forces that continually shape it. The significance of Kore-eda's films, this book argues, is not found in their capacity to subvert these systems or to produce activist characters who can stand outside of them; rather, it is found in their contradictory attempt to locate a sense of human expression within a larger nonanthropocentric worldview. Acknowledging the inevitable constraints that determine and shape the characters that populate his documentaries and feature films, Kore-eda is able to locate humanity in the surpluses of desire that result from living, connecting, and moving within the systems acting on them. These very human excesses allow his characters' interactions to temporarily reframe a sense of community and identity, helping audiences experience moments of intimacy that linger once the bodies of his characters pass through the shared space of the camera frame.

Notes

1. Adam Bingham, among others, argues that Kore-eda is known for incorporating elements of classical Japanese culture into his work (8–11).

2. Film critic Donald Richie notes that the cinematic techniques used to relay the "bare story" of a young widow who grapples with her husband's suicide "are deliberately kept at a minimum" (38).

3. The austerity that critics recognize in Kore-eda's films is less a manifestation of Buddhist values, I argue, and more the effect of the volatility of neoliberal influence on social relations.

4. The two mediums differ in their focus: documentaries seek to capture specific social or political problems that lead to abstract conclusions or ques-

tions, while fiction moves in the opposite direction, from abstractions to specifics (Paletz and Saito 54).

5. Kore-eda made a documentary on Taiwanese directors Hou Hsiao-hsien and Edward Yang during his time at TV Man.

6. However, Kore-eda does suggest that anger is the central emotion behind *Shoplifters*.

7. One temptation is to attribute the nonanthropocentric agency of Kore-eda's characters to native philosophical perspectives in which humans are viewed as part of the larger natural order, not as outside it. Applying this framework to Kore-eda's work ignores the impact of the socioeconomic systems that form a more pertinent epistemological framework for evaluating Kore-eda's films, a framework that applies not just to Asian traditions but also to other developed nations around the world.

8. Kore-eda formed his own production company in 2014.

9. In recent years, Kore-eda has worked with a handful of non-Japanese actors and crew members, including South Korean actress Bae Doona on *Air Doll* and *Broker* and Taiwanese cinematographer Ping Bin Lee on *Air Doll*. Even more recently, he has ventured out of his comfort zone, working on international film sets in France and South Korea. He spent over a month shooting *The Truth* in Paris, during which time he worked solely with French and American actors, including Deneuve, Binoche, and Ethan Hawke. Although the only Japanese nationals on the set included a producer and a food stylist (Hori and Kore-eda 27), Kore-eda did not experience much difference between French and Japanese film sets (Arai 19).

10. The fact that the "sex scene" in *Air Doll* happens in the adult section of the video store suggests a connection between filmmaking and learning. This moment influences one of the final shots in *After Life*, when Takashi finally chooses a memory of his time working on the film set at the way station.

11. Kore-eda often focuses on the people behind the camera, drawing them into the experiences and memories portrayed in *After Life* and *The Truth*.

12. The physical changes that child actors experience during the shooting of Kore-eda's films are often incorporated into the films themselves. When the actor playing Yuri in *Shoplifters*, Sasaki Miyu, lost one of her teeth in production, Kore-eda wrote it in as part of the film.

13. The only exception to LDP rule was from 1993 to 1994 and 2009 to 2012.

14. Indeed, actor Rirī Furankī, who plays the part of Osamu in *Shoplifters*, argues that the film manifests a sense of anger toward the regulation of the family in contemporary Japan (Rirī and Kore-eda, "Egakō" 20).

15. James Roberson notes that the socioeconomic conditions experienced by working-class families in Japan do not conform to those of the ideal family imagined by the state (128).

16. The family structure in *Shoplifters* is reflected in more fantastic terms in *Air Doll*, in which the "wife" (sex doll) is literally a product of the economic

system—the protagonist can easily replace her, like replacing one object for an identical one. Although the theme of the interchangeability of familial networks is most prominent in *Shoplifters*, it manifests more subtly in earlier films such as *Distance*, in which a young man, Atsushi, visits an elderly man in the hospital so often that attendants think he is the man's son, when in reality he is not.

17. While *Our Little Sister* shows audiences the complexity of female networks, other Kore-eda films explore masculine roles in society. As will be discussed in more detail in the next section, the traditional roles of male figures are often reimagined in films such as *The Truth*. Although the film centers on the duel between Fabienne and Lumir, Hank, a second-rate actor, joins the cadre of men who serve these two women by preparing their food, tracking their appointments, and keeping them company.

18. Film critic Kinbara Yuka suggests that the type of father who does not just "play a role" in the family but is present and active as a parent is replacing the distant father figure from previous generations (Todoroki and Kinbara 57).

19. Founded in 1984 by Asahara (b. 2 March 1955 as Chizuo Matsumoto) as a yoga and meditation group, Aum gradually grew in size and influence, developing a utopian vision of Japan that it sought to realize through violence. Aum began to see its mission as saving Japan from global threats such as the United States and initially sought to carry out its goals through political persuasion. When its attempts to win seats in the 1990 general election failed, the group turned to violence, seeking to "force an end" and carry out Armageddon. Beginning in the late 1980s, Aum was involved in several terrorist activities, including kidnappings and murders, leading up to the gas attacks in 1995. The attacks in Tokyo were the first step in a larger plan to save the world from spiritual decay by taking over the government and replacing officials with Aum's own leaders.

20. These two characters are referred to by their surname in the film.

21. If the Shibata home transforms Yuri's body, the house itself is transformed, as Yuri resides with the Shibatas for several months. When one of Yuri's teeth falls out, the family throws it onto the roof of the home, according to Japanese tradition. Later, Yuri helps the family bury Hatsue's body in the home's entranceway after Hatsue dies in her sleep, further demonstrating ways in which physical bodies and locations become one.

22. In a shot that recalls the truck ride in *Distance*, the children in *I Wish*, with their bodies bumping up and down and their hair blowing in the breeze, hitch a ride in the back of a flatbed to the place where they will see bullet trains.

23. The few times that Kore-eda uses flashbacks are limited to his early films, including *Maborosi*; *Nobody Knows*, which opens in medias res, so the whole film becomes a flashback; and *I Wish*, in which a single flashback reveals the tension-filled family dynamic that led to the parents' divorce and the two brothers' separation.

24. These cassettes provide a prompt for Ichirō's memory rather than an archive in and of themselves. Susannah Radstone argues that memory texts

supplement other forms of memory: "Like images from the family album, home movies supplement, enhance or even supplant intimate memories of the personal and familial past" (328).

25. The relationship between the neutral footage on the video tapes and the re-creation of these moments on the set demonstrates the interaction between documentary and feature filmmaking in Kore-eda's own work.

26. Memory as a punishment is a theme in *The Third Murder*. Memory, just like Misumi's jail cell, becomes a way to control Misumi. He is a prisoner of the memory of Shigemori's father, who tried Misumi's first murder case thirty years ago and believes that Misumi is a natural-born killer. Indeed, being imprisoned by the memories of others keeps Misumi from acting in the present and protecting his boss's teenage daughter, Sakie, who was being abused by her father.

Interviews with Kore-eda Hirokazu |

During the process of writing this book, I had the opportunity to correspond with Kore-eda through his assistant, and I inquired about the possibility of including translations of some of Kore-eda's interviews in Japanese in the manuscript. While we discussed which interviews would be most applicable to the book, Kore-eda expressed concern that some of his earlier interviews no longer reflect his way of thinking and style of filmmaking. In the end, we agreed that it would be best to include three interviews given at different points over the course of his career to reflect the different stages of his development as a filmmaker while illustrating some of the enduring themes of his films, including the technical and formal aspects of documentary and feature filmmaking, his exploration of the nature and function of families, and his interest in social engagement. I translated all three of the following interviews and am reproducing them here with permission.

"Kamera wo hasande, tagai ga seicho shite iku" (Those on both
sides of the camera can grow), by Shimamori Michiko

"Umi yori mo fukaku: Mō soko ni inai kazoku wo egaku" (*After the
Storm*: Depicting a family that is no longer there), by Ogawa
Yōko

"Rirī Furankī, kazoku no naka no chichi, Osamu, Kore-eda Hirokazu kantoku ga 10 nenkan kangaete kita koto, ikkannsei ga
arata na ryōiki e fumidasu" (Rirī Furankī, the father of the family, Osamu, director Kore-eda Hirokazu takes a step into new
territory after ten years), by Todoroki Yukio et al.

Given around the time of the release of his third feature, *Distance*
(2001), "Those on Both Sides of the Camera Can Grow" is the first of
three interviews that Kore-eda gave with Shimamori Michiko, who is a
critic, essayist, and the former editor in chief of the monthly advertis-
ing magazine *Advertisement Criticism*. The interview was originally
published in May 2001 in *Advertisement Criticism* but was reprinted
as part of a special volume on the films of Kore-eda Hirokazu, *Kore-
eda Hirokazu: Mata koko kara hajimaru* (Kore-eda Hirokazu: Starting
from this point again), edited by Sen Misa and published by Kawade
Books, one of Japan's leading publishers, in 2017. I chose this interview because it provides insight into the role that Kore-eda's training
in documentary filmmaking plays in the making of his feature films. To
tone down emotion and to add complexity to the conventional stories
in his more contemporary feature films, Kore-eda continues to rely on
the style of documentary filmmaking: handheld cameras, naturalistic
lighting, and a spare sound design, aspects that characterize the style of
Kore-eda's early features such as *Distance*, *After Life*, *Nobody Knows*,
and others. Even in his most commercial films—*I Wish* and *Our Little
Sister*—Kore-eda pulled back to capture exchanges between characters
in wide shots or from behind. The naturalism of the observational style
of his early features reemerged in *Shoplifters*, in which he reused the
question-and-answer sessions that characterize *After Life*; *I Wish*; *Like
Father, Like Son*; and *The Truth*, which is perhaps the closest to a remake
of *After Life*. The interview's discussion deals primarily with Kore-eda's
first three films (*Maborosi*, *After Life*, and *Distance*) but also delves
into his early work on television documentaries for *Nonfix*, including

However . . . in the Time of Government Aid Cuts and *This Is How I'm Living with AIDS—Hirata Yutaka Recounts.*

"Those on Both Sides of the Camera Can Grow," by Shimamori Michiko

Between Perpetrator and Victim

SHIMAMORI: First off, can I ask you about the timing of shooting *Distance* (2001)? I imagine that it took some time to warm up to the project after the subway gas attacks.

KORE-EDA: Actually, I was in the middle of editing a film when the attacks occurred and chose to focus on my work, deliberately avoiding the incident for a while. The fact that members of my generation were at the center of the event piqued my curiosity, but it didn't go any further than that, or rather, I didn't let it go any further. After I heard the news of Jōyū Fumihiro's [the former spokesperson of Aum] release from jail while I was working on the plot of a new film around the end of the year two years ago, vague ideas about portraying the media and its role in the event, about capturing the dark side of humanity, and about thematizing the idea of fiction came to mind.

SHIMAMORI: So that was the timing? Just to confirm, this was in 1999?

KORE-EDA: The end of 1999.

SHIMAMORI: So, rather than a concrete image, you had a theme and concept in mind at that point?

KORE-EDA: Yes, and along with that I wanted to take the methodology I used with *After Life* (1998) one step further, hoping to once again rely on the emotion and performances generated on set as I worked with the cast without a fully formed screenplay. That is all I knew for sure. Watching the broadcast, I thought about the grand narratives that we create (such as "religion" and "god"), whether they are true or not, and how I can burden the main characters with the darkness these narratives bring. As I mulled over these ideas, the story suddenly took off.

SHIMAMORI: The film's focus on the "family of the perpetrators" caught me off guard a little. It was compelling but also a bit hard to swallow. The tendency is to go with the "victim's" perspective or a relatable point of view. However, focusing on the perspective of the "perpetrators" can also yield new insights.

KORE-EDA: Probably because I worked in television for so long, all I would see on news reports, in particular, were clearly defined character types: the "evil criminal," the "innocent murder victim," and the "bereaved family." If you have these three types, you're good—all there is left is to uncover the crime. However, real life is more complex. If all they see, sitting in front of the TV, is a world in which the line between good and evil is so clearly defined, the viewer can be nothing more than a third-person spectator. It's easy for spectators who become emotionally invested to embrace the bereaved family's perspective and cast blame on the perpetrator because they have no skin in the game. I wanted to create characters who, first and foremost, do not conform to that pattern, characters whom you never see on television, ones that are difficult to feature. And along with that, I wanted to deal with the duality of the idea of "perpetrator" and "victim," a seemingly peculiar concept, yet one that you must accept living in contemporary Japan. Considering that most are not totally comfortable with a black-and-white reality, focusing on the family of the perpetrators, I thought, would help expose this condition.

SHIMAMORI: The process of making the film after the plot was formed is interesting. I'd love to hear in greater detail about its development.

KORE-EDA: As we turned to casting after completing the general story arc of the film, the character types of the four or five main leads were still not completely formed, so we focused on building the characters with the cast. We spent the next few months sketching the characters, deciding on their professions, the type of homes in which they lived, as well as the professions and the personalities of the deceased with whom these main characters had relationships as siblings and as spouses.

SHIMAMORI: You fleshed out the specifics of the characters during that time. So the initial story arc you came up with had the family members of the perpetrators assemble somehow?

KORE-EDA: They were to gather, take a trip, and for some reason be unable to return home, spending one night with a former believer of the group and then leaving—that much was decided. But we had to figure out what happened during that process. At first it was a more complicated story involving several encounters, including one with an elderly couple who were in the mountains to commit suicide, but we eventually gave up on that whole idea.

SHIMAMORI: Why did you give up on it?

KORE-EDA: When we thought more about how their personal issues and grief would come to the surface through their encounters with people at the mountain lodge, it seemed like having to finally deal with the thoughts and memories they had buried deep in their soul would make for a more painful stay than these outward interactions. When I came up with the "recollection" structure of the film, in which the memories of the last time the main characters saw their family members would be portrayed, everything else in the story seemed unnecessary. So I started from scratch and reworked the story around that idea.

Creating through Destruction

SHIMAMORI: This seems like a film that was determined largely by casting, by whom you decided to put in certain roles.

KORE-EDA: Yes. I'm not just saying this, but [the film's success] was all thanks to the cast. The amount of tension we were able to create in the film with this subject matter and style of shooting was solely due to our success in casting the film. Without a doubt.

SHIMAMORI: Did you really sleep over at the location with the cast and crew?

KORE-EDA: Yes, at a bed-and-breakfast next to the lake in the Nagano prefecture.

SHIMAMORI: How many days?

KORE-EDA: Ten days on-site. Ten days, starting from the time we arrived.

SHIMAMORI: Did you shoot the film in chronological order?

KORE-EDA: It took a week to shoot the nighttime scene in the mountains, so we didn't shoot in chronological order, but we didn't jump around too much either. I'm not one who can start shooting a film with the last scene. Scenes would change as we shot them, so the continuity suffered when we shot them separately [*laughs*].

SHIMAMORI: Did the film change much as you shot it?

KORE-EDA: It did. Scenes shot on location would turn out surprisingly good—so natural that they seemed like they were designed beforehand when in reality they were often written on-site. The scene at the beginning in which Arata and Isseya (Yūsuke) walk down the tracks toward the station, looking up at the lilies, was captured when we jumped out of our car on the way to another location, and the scene in which Asano (Tadanobu) and Ryō yell "yahoo!" at the pier was shot when they both happened to be free one day and I took them to the site.

SHIMAMORI: This is not the first time you used this style of shooting, right?

KORE-EDA: Shooting *After Life*, I intentionally broke many rules and learned that it worked for me, so this time I had a clear plan. Arata and Isseya knew that this was the way the production would go from the start [*laughs*].

SHIMAMORI: It must have been good to have those two along. Isseya is somewhat of a—

KORE-EDA: There's no way to describe him [*laughs*]. He is unlike anyone I have ever worked with.

SHIMAMORI: Performance and real life blend together with him. It's tough to see the difference between the two.

KORE-EDA: Even he doesn't know the difference [*laughs*]. Of course, there's a character there—he's not just playing himself. I gathered the four main actors together on the first day of rehearsals and, after having them introduce themselves, asked them to try to act as their character for fun—ready, go. But Isseya alone continued to talk in the same way, as if nothing happened. At that point, Natsukawa (Kiyoka) suddenly stopped talking. But that was natural for her—she had never spoken in front of the camera, except when delivering actual lines. But Isseya would ask her questions and prod her like normal. So I relied on Isseya to help Natsukawa overcome her inhibitions during the first part of the film. Halfway through, I mentioned to her that she had changed, but she realized this was okay and had a lot of fun with it after that.

SHIMAMORI: It was the type of complex performance you'd expect of a great actor.

KORE-EDA: It was. The number of directors who make films largely on a set has increased. Directors such as Endō Ken'ichi skip rehearsal and start shooting on the very first day the cast meets, calling it a day when they're satisfied with what they have [*laughs*].

SHIMAMORI: Do you provide lines in the script?

KORE-EDA: Not actual lines but conditions or even situations, such as how Endō and Natsukawa became a couple: they were classmates at college. After they learned these aspects of their backstory, I told Natsukawa to refuse her husband's invitations to come with him to the "other side" out of a sense of self-protection in the scene when they are standing together on the veranda of their apartment. The key phrase in that exchange was "you've changed." I asked that she use this one phrase as a trigger for her character to reflect on which one of them had changed over the past several years. I instructed her to refuse her husband's persuasions like she herself would as a wife trying to maintain her happy home. I gave each cast member these types of instructions but left the flow of the scene up to them.

SHIMAMORI: You can get a sense of this same technique in *After Life* during the scene about betting.

KORE-EDA: If I can help the staff and cast understand what I am trying to do in a particular scene from the start, it often exceeds my expectations. Of course, there are scenes that don't go so well and need to be cut, but for the most part scenes turn out better than I expect [*laughs*].

SHIMAMORI: It seems like the reality of the words would be different from traditional acting.

KORE-EDA: This is the feeling I get at shooting locations. In a normal sense, the cameramen would struggle if they did not know how the actors were going to move. But because the cameramen that I worked with had primarily shot documentaries up to that point, for them movement is natural, and having things choreographed is actually harder to shoot. Sound was recorded from the side of their cameras.

SHIMAMORI: That seems like the way things are done in television and in documentaries.

KORE-EDA: Yes, it's the method used by sound engineers for documentaries. There was only one microphone, so capturing five people speaking was challenging, but it was more interesting for my sound guy than if the order of the dialogue had been decided in advance.

SHIMAMORI: Did you only use one mic when the five actors were all together too?

KORE-EDA: We used wireless mics during the scene at Shinjuku station because of the background noise, but other than that it was just one mic. At first, it was going to be just a small road movie with Arata and Isseya, so my staff had that type of film in mind when they joined the production, but before we knew it, the cast grew to five, and the technical staff complained that they had been tricked [*laughs*].

SHIMAMORI: Did you intend for it to be that way?

KORE-EDA: I did [*laughs*]. I told everyone there would be no costume or art directors on set, so just come with the clothes on your back and have fun with it. The cameraman, sound people, and assistant directors were all on board with the plan. My third assistant director on *After Life*—with whom I had never worked before that film—came on as assistant director for *Distance*.

SHIMAMORI: As assistant director?

KORE-EDA: She was in charge, but she was probably the one who felt most deceived. However, the shooting style of *After Life* was her first experience with filmmaking, so, being familiar with film sets on which things were not perfectly planned out, she proved to be very flexible in adapting to the situation. On a set like that, where we couldn't afford any mistakes by the staff, having someone incapable of getting the job done would have really sunk us, so miraculously, everything went well.

SHIMAMORI: Ryō also did a great job.

KORE-EDA: She had worked primarily in serial dramas and always wanted to try something like this, so she had a lot of fun. There were no written lines for her scene with Arata; it was mostly generated by them. Because Arata really got what I was trying to do in the film, I left most of it up to him. The story he told about the lonely bird was something he came up with on his own without instruction from me.

SHIMAMORI: Everyone took on the role of scriptwriter [*laughs*].

KORE-EDA: Everyone took it upon themselves to build on my vision. When I was editing a scene in which the sound of a river made it hard for me to hear the dialogue on-site, I didn't know until the editing phase what [the actors] were actually talking about [*laughs*].

SHIMAMORI: That's funny. But that was probably necessary for them to take a step forward—they really had to inhabit their roles. They had to act on their own.

KORE-EDA: You can call it duplicitous if you like.

Maborosi Lacked Excitement

SHIMAMORI: I don't think it was duplicitous, but given the traditional view of the director as the one with complete control over the world of the film, whether it was premeditated or not, it's still an audacious move.

KORE-EDA: In making *Maborosi* (1995), I tried to control every frame in that way. I meticulously planned the continuity, including every cut, along with the soundscape of the film, working with a highly competent technical staff who really understood my vision and worked to realize it. The final product, however, lacked a sense of life, like a static picture of the images in my mind.

SHIMAMORI: You don't think it was more than that?

KORE-EDA: Yes. In other words, I didn't get excited on set—I was just putting the finishing touches on the picture in my mind. Of course, I'm thankful to that film; it was a positive step in my career, one that allowed me to make my second and third films, but there was something lacking on my part. At one point, I thought there was something wrong and even considered starting over from scratch. I first began working with the visual image on television documentaries. My process of making a film involved shooting interview subjects whose responses, or sometimes lack thereof, would often completely defy the expectations I had in preparing for the interviews. This back-and-forth with interview subjects engaged me mentally and emotionally as I made each program. These sessions were by far the most interesting part of making documentaries, really enriching the process for me. So whether it's an actor or a regular person, you develop a relationship with the subject on the other side of the camera, using what you get from the exchange in the next interview or scene. But as I sought to reverse course on my work on *Maborosi*, I wondered, could this process of mutual growth work in making feature films too?

SHIMAMORI: In that sense, the methodology and concept of *After Life* are interesting.

KORE-EDA: The screenplay for *After Life* was completed when I was twenty-seven years old as a fully formed script with all the dialogue included. I totally scrapped it to make the film.

SHIMAMORI: So the idea of being able to carry one memory with you to the other side was already in your mind?

KORE-EDA: It was originally a story about the deceased meeting in one location, watching a film about their lives, and choosing one moment before going to heaven—in other words, it was from the perspective of the deceased. In the process of adapting it into a film, I changed the perspective to that of the people who work at this location. The impetus for the film was based on my experiences at the beginning of my career in television when I was still an assistant director of travel and quiz shows. Returning from shoots, directors would go straight home while assistants headed off with the footage to the editing room to produce the script. I would make note of the questions and answers given during interviews and the different backgrounds while working endlessly by myself to keep track of the time codes. One night while I was working alone in the editing room, I imagined a scene with a room like the one in which I was working, in which you are shown a row of numbered video tapes as you pass through after death.

SHIMAMORI: Nonactors were mixed in with the cast playing the deceased, right?

KORE-EDA: Half were nonactors.

SHIMAMORI: How did you handle the talkative ones?

KORE-EDA: I would let them talk as long as they liked [*laughs*].

SHIMAMORI: All of them? Wow, you're a saint. Letting people talk for as long as they like would be more realistic, but the camera is rolling all that time, right?

KORE-EDA: Probably because these are their treasured stories, right?

SHIMAMORI: You surely can't have a script in that case. Did someone ask the questions?

KORE-EDA: Yes, just like the setup in the film: the deceased sat on one side of the table and [there was] a worker like Arata on the other side, with me next to them asking questions.

SHIMAMORI: Surely, if you ask them questions, they're going to respond.

KORE-EDA: We would ask questions such as "What kinds of shoes were you wearing in your memory?" It was amusing when nonactors would relay their memories, but when they stepped onto the stage where these memories would be re-created on film, they would get confused, like the woman who forgot what to do with her handkerchief as she started to dance to the song "Red Shoes." With or without the camera, I feel like it was my job on the set to elicit those spontaneous performances. Another fun moment was when one of the actors was inspired by an elderly woman to join her in singing. I realized how great it is to be an actor.

SHIMAMORI: So there weren't really roles? It was more organic?

KORE-EDA: It mostly came out organically. The interactions on set really allowed for a great shooting environment in which the confluence of seemingly incompatible forces inspired one another amid the cacophonous voices of the nonprofessionals. I thought how great it would be if I could draw out these kinds of performances in making a film. That was probably the turning point for me. If I didn't find these performances interesting, I would have returned to shooting the nonactors.

SHIMAMORI: I see. So the nonactors were also great. But if you consider nonactors to be interesting just because they are regular people, it would have turned out differently.

KORE-EDA: I think so.

SHIMAMORI: You're making a documentary too, but if you continue along this path, you lose a sense of the difference between documentary and fiction.

KORE-EDA: Definitely. Just because I'm shooting regular people, it doesn't mean it's a documentary. I have a variety of ways to capture a subject, one being a documentary approach, which is how you might characterize the methodology of *Distance*. Yet you can also call the final product fiction.

SHIMAMORI: In other words, our understanding of the nature of fiction is inevitably changing. If it doesn't change, maybe we will lose a sense of the real.

KORE-EDA: I agree. We started making films in the wake of the destruction of the system perfected by the studios. I understand the joy of watching classic Japanese cinema: impeccable filmmaking technique, film art that reaches ideal levels, and beautiful actors on-stage. Yet while I am impressed with the splendor of this closed-off dream world, we have no way of reproducing it and no way to enjoy disconnecting from reality. It's inevitable, then, that filmmakers from our generation would seek to create a very different sense of reality through the fictional medium of film and that there would be people drawn to this new reality.

SHIMAMORI: Surely, it is possible to portray truth through fiction. If that's the case, it seems that the notion that documentary filmmaking was the start to this process has a large impact on you today.

KORE-EDA: Yes, a very large one.

I Want to Be Socially Engaged

SHIMAMORI: You made some ambitious and critically acclaimed works during your documentary period, right?

KORE-EDA: I was making documentaries during the early 1990s, when Fuji Television was still producing experimental late-night programming. They had an hour-long show called *Nonfix*, and they pretty much allowed me to do what I wanted. My projects were green lit with just the approval of Kanamitsu Osamu and Ogawa Shinichi, the two "late-night managers," as they were known.

SHIMAMORI: Those were good times, I'm sure.

KORE-EDA: Yes, they were. I worked there for three or four years. I'm not known for being a prolific director. At the most, I made three or four films a year.

SHIMAMORI: This might be a strange way of saying this, but you seem to be part of the "socially engaged set" in that you make films with the intent of merging human interest and social concerns, something that is rare in the younger generation [*laughs*].

KORE-EDA: I'm not conscious of it, but that could be an initial approach to my work. The first thing I was slated to make at *Nonfix* was a film about the suicide of Yamanouchi Toyonori, a bureaucrat from the Ministry of the Environment who was responsible for handling the litigation over compensation for Minamata disease, and two women who killed themselves due to the cancellation of their welfare benefits. Focusing on the theme of benefit cuts, I conducted interviews centered on the suicide of these two women, putting together a film that was supposed to be about the mishandling of entitlements by bureaucrats. However, as I was conducting interviews, Mr. Yamanouchi committed suicide, and a quick examination of his background revealed that he held the post of chief of social affairs in the Ministry of Health, Labour and Welfare. He piqued my interest as someone who might be responsible for some of the problems in the administration of social affairs. Digging deeper, I learned that he graduated with a law degree from Tokyo University and placed second on the civil service examination, which put him on an elite path to join the Ministry of Finance or the Ministry of Foreign Affairs. But I also learned that he submitted a piece about the problems with welfare administration to a newspaper under a false name, implicating the Social Welfare Bureau and disability welfare before he was ultimately relocated to the Ministry of the Environment. At first, my plan was to create a simplistic story that pitted evil bureaucrats against helpless victims, but when I came upon this tortured bureaucrat whose struggle led him to commit suicide, I was reminded of the narrow-mindedness of my attempts to force people into conventional and hackneyed story lines.

SHIMAMORI: You made an appearance in the film you shot about the AIDS patient [Hirata], right?

KORE-EDA: Yes, I was pulled into the film by him, but I used the experience of getting pulled in in the making of the film itself. Making documentaries is not about capturing anything as lofty as "truth" but about depicting the shared time and relationships between those on the opposite sides of the camera. As I began to realize this, I recognized that those moments when interview subjects look at the camera or talk to me while I'm sitting next to it—the moments that I would scuttle in editing when I first started making films—really contain the essence of the documentary medium. The man you are talking about, Mr. Hirata, was the type of guy who would call you up just because he wanted someone to talk to, and when you got to his place he would vent his frustrations at everyone until he felt better and then want to get something to eat [*laughs*]. So we intentionally made our getting pulled into the story the subplot.

SHIMAMORI: Did you have any reservations about appearing in the show?

KORE-EDA: I did at first, but they disappeared after the program was finished. But I did worry about it during shooting.

SHIMAMORI: So there was a point when you got over your doubts?

KORE-EDA: There was, but we were also getting criticized. There were those who thought that we shouldn't be part of the program. He [Hirata] gradually began to lose his eyesight and at one point dropped his medicine on the ground. I was there by myself and didn't pick it up for him but continued to shoot him fumbling around for it. I finally picked it up and gave it to him, but we really got criticized for that. In other words, is it okay to shoot him while he is struggling to pick up the medicine? There is that way of thinking. But before anything else, I would want to do the normal things that human beings do and not forget what it's like to do them.

SHIMAMORI: Did you join TV Man Union because you wanted to make documentaries?

KORE-EDA: I didn't. At first, I just wanted to make films. I had worked as an assistant director on travel and international interview shows, and there was a part of me that couldn't stand it anymore, so they allowed me to quit making regular programming. After that, my first project was a proposal on Mr. Yamanouchi. The pitch was about social awareness, but the finished product was about human frailty. In that way, the finished product deviated from the starting point, but that deviation was not a bad thing in my mind [*laughs*].

SHIMAMORI: You were able to produce good work early on. In the end, you're a journalist, aren't you? Your next film, *Distance*, was also journalistic, though it would differ from the original meaning of the word.

KORE-EDA: It also seems journalistic to me, but I really don't like the implication of the words *social engagement* and *journalism*, so I don't use them myself. But I also don't want to forget my own socially engaged perspective. Improvements in the quality of home video have made it possible to film anything on your own these days, increasing interest in filmmaking, but there are many young people who still struggle to point their camera at other people. Because they struggle to build a connection with those on the other side of the camera, they focus on those with whom they have a preexisting relationship—family, lovers, and themselves. They turn inward, not out, leading to a polarized reaction involving either social withdrawal or violence directed at the world around them. If they don't learn how to shoot a film by talking face-to-face like this, they won't experience any growth through documentary filmmaking.

SHIMAMORI: The world becomes distorted, and their self-aggrandizement takes on strange proportions. Do you feel like you grow as you shoot films?

KORE-EDA: I realized how I've grown once I've shot a film. I tend toward social withdrawal [*laughs*], but when I first picked up a camera, conversely, I found I was able to have relationships with other people and discovered that I can continue to grow.

SHIMAMORI: My final question is about how "quiet" your films are. Our discussion about microphones was revealing, but the overall tone of your films is uniquely quiet. Is that part of your nature as a filmmaker?

KORE-EDA: The parts that feel quiet are probably due to my nature. In particular, the scene construction and sound design of this current film are probably the most naturalistic of all my work. Concerning sound design, when I watch other people's films, my sense of discomfort stems from the disproportionate loudness of the sound captured by the mic during long shots. I didn't get this right in *Maborosi*. Ideally, the distance of the subject should equal the distance of the sound. I aimed to fix it in *After Life*—capturing sound at camera distance.

SHIMAMORI: Is it okay if it's difficult to hear or if you can't hear at all?

KORE-EDA: Yes, I think so.

SHIMAMORI: This is the way most people perceive things. Without thinking, we sometimes perk up our ears. Images help, but often subtle sensations that are hard to express in words arise from the environment, like the sound of the wind. This is one of the most powerful parts of your films.

KORE-EDA: I didn't use much music for this film, so by the end your ears are probably the most tired they have ever been [*laughs*]. Music puts viewers at ease because it is comforting. So getting rid of music allows ambient sounds to overflow, and your ears pick up on all of them.

SHIMAMORI: Is there a specific reason you have become so conscious of sound?

KORE-EDA: As we discussed with *Maborosi*, I wanted to capture the voices of the actors, so I stuck a pin mic on Emoto Akira and Esumi Makiko when they were talking on the shore by the fire, close to the end of the film. The scene was captured with a long shot, so you shouldn't be able to hear waves or anything else. Watching Victor Erice's *The Spirit of the Beehive* and *El Sur*, with their simple sound design, I was led to reconsider: If I were shooting the film now, would I leave out the sound of the waves? Or if I wanted to have that sound, how would I try to capture it in a different way? When I want to hear soft voices, I'll move closer. The proximity is based perfectly on the distance of the sound. I was never able to get comfortable with it. But once I realized you can create sound design with such a simple approach, I stopped trying so hard.

"*After the Storm*: Depicting a Family That Is No Longer There," by Ogawa Yōko

This interview involved a discussion between Kore-eda and Japanese novelist Ogawa Yōko that occurred upon the release of Kore-eda's eleventh film, *After the Storm*. The interview was published in Japan's leading film magazine, *Kinema Junpō*. Themes of family and memory in Ogawa's most well known work, *The Housekeeper and the Professor* (*Hakase no ai shita sūshiki*, 2003), are inspired by Kore-eda's films, including his documentary *Without Memory* (1996). The conversation provides insight into Kore-eda's work with child actors and the role his own personal experiences play in his films. It also touches on works throughout Kore-eda's career, including *Lessons from a Calf*, *Nobody Knows*, *Still Walking*, *Our Little Sister*, and *After the Storm*.

MODERATOR: The opening of *After the Storm* is on May 21. In this film, Kore-eda's memories from his youth are on display in many forms. Though it's only fiction, filmmaking took place in the apartment complex in which Kore-eda lived until he was twenty-eight. Today we have the pleasure of hearing a discussion between Kore-eda, who commuted to college from this same *danchi*, and writer Ogawa Yōko, who was a student at this same time. Born the same year, 1962, they both majored in literature at Waseda University. Ogawa requested this interview with Kore-eda and claims that "I had no idea it would ever happen." This is their first time meeting. They never met as students.

KORE-EDA: We both graduated from the Department of Literature.

OGAWA: Really? What did you write your thesis on?

KORE-EDA: Film professor Iwamoto Kenji allowed me to write a screenplay in place of a thesis. I originally thought I could make a living writing second-rate novels, so I joined the literary arts section of the Department of Literature.

OGAWA: Is that so? But since you wrote a screenplay as your graduate thesis, you must have already caught a glimpse of what you wanted to become.

KORE-EDA: I wonder [*laughs*]. But I did skip out on classes and practically lived in movie theaters once I entered college [*laughs*]. My interest shifted from novels to screen plays, and I even started going to a scriptwriting school. So, either way, I wanted to be a writer of some kind.

OGAWA: A while ago, you shot the documentary for NHK about the family struggling with Wernicke-Korsakoff syndrome (*Without Memory*). That was the first time I heard your name. In fact, that film served as inspiration for my novel *The Housekeeper and the Professor*.

KORE-EDA: Really? That's nice to hear.

OGAWA: The scene in which the husband looks curiously at the pink baby clothes hanging out to dry, forgetting that he has a baby girl, was unforgettable. You caught the husband crying every morning when his wife told him his condition, filming through the sliding door.

KORE-EDA: You really noticed those details.

OGAWA: It's unusual for me, but I can remember everything from that scene. That's why I always felt an affinity toward you [*laughs*].

KORE-EDA: I appreciate that. During college, I really wanted to make films but also couldn't shake the desire to write. At the time, I was working part-time as a tutor for Fukutake Publishing (currently Benesse Corporation) [a company that focuses on correspondence education and publishing]. With that connection I got hired into the publishing side of Fukutake. My goal was to join the editorial team of *Kaien* [a weekly literary magazine published by Fukutake and Benesse], and while editing the magazine, I would write novels, win *Kaien*'s New Writer Prize, next win the Akutagawa Prize, quit editing, and so forth. That was my personal plan [*laughs*].

OGAWA: That's a very specific plan [*laughs*].

KORE-EDA: A plan I failed to execute. Coincidentally, you followed this same plan with success, earning *Kaien*'s New Writer Prize and the Akutagawa Prize and graduating the same year from the same department and university. I didn't really want to win the Akutagawa Prize—or maybe I did. But either way, you were able to go where I wanted to. There is no way to know if you were inspired by my documentary, as you mentioned, but the first time I read *The Housekeeper and the Professor*, I realized why you had such a deep understanding of it. I feel like we must be connected somehow.

OGAWA: This is crazy, but I also worked at Fukutake as a tutor [*laughs*].

KORE-EDA: Really!?!

OGAWA: Yes, and I took the company entrance examination for Fukutake but failed. So our connection goes back that far.

KORE-EDA: Maybe we ran into each other there.

OGAWA: I was a tutor for writing essays.

KORE-EDA: So was I.

OGAWA: Really [*laughs*]? Failing the entrance exam gave me the drive to prove them wrong and shoot for the *Kaien* New Writer Prize [*laughs*].

KORE-EDA: Wow. I'm shocked [*laughs*].

OGAWA: But it must have been competitive to get into TV Man Union too, right?

KORE-EDA: Yes, but they were the only ones that accepted me. I failed everywhere else [*laughs*]. It seems like they gave saucy candidates like me a chance during those days, particularly those that talked back during their recruitment interview, like me [*laughs*].

Why Are You Drawn to Children?

OGAWA: With films such as *Nobody Knows* (2004), as with novels, children are hidden gems. Since they still don't grasp language perfectly, they have no guile. So there's still a lot they can't express in words. I suppose novels and films are the means to give voice to these things. What is the origin of your interest in children?

KORE-EDA: Maybe it's because I wanted to become a teacher, or, more precisely, I was told to become one. The mother in *After the Storm* talks about "public servants" over and over, but when I had to do another year in school and delay graduation, my mother's one condition for paying my school fees was that I would get my teaching credentials.

OGAWA: Your mother had a great way of motivating you [*laughs*].

KORE-EDA: I couldn't graduate after my fourth year because I didn't go to class during my second and third years, so I got my teaching credentials and even did some student teaching, but I talked back again [*laughs*].

OGAWA: Talked back to whom [*laughs*]—your academic advisor?

KORE-EDA: Yes, I am much easier going these days—I don't know why I got into so many confrontations back then [*laughs*]. Anyway, because my grades with student teaching were poor, I gave up on trying to get my license [*laughs*]. Partly for that reason, I shot a documentary in my twenties about a school in Nagano, *Lessons from a Calf* (1991). I visited the integrative learning school for three years as an independent filmmaker, and you can say that was the basis [for my interest in working with children].

OGAWA: Oh, integrated learning, like raising livestock and milking cows?

KORE-EDA: The fun I had capturing the children on film really opened my eyes.

OGAWA: Talking about children reminds me of the wonderful performance by the character of the son (Yoshizawa Taiyō) in *After the Storm*. His face seems to suggest that he knows much more than his parents think.

KORE-EDA: Ever since meeting him at the audition, I thought there was something special about him. He was so quiet, even when acting [*laughs*]. Most of the children who come from the agency greet us enthusiastically with a loud voice that grabs us, "Good morning!" But he was so quiet that you'd have to get close to hear him. His head was shaved for another show in a way that he didn't like, and his discomfort worked well for the part.

OGAWA: What a fortuitous meeting. In the film, when he must go to dinner with his mother and her boyfriend (Ozawa Yukiyoshi), his expression shows that he is reluctantly doing it for his mother (Maki Yōko), even though he really doesn't want to.

KORE-EDA: He was the most grown up of all the characters in the film [*laughs*].

OGAWA: Perhaps. In other words, the adults around him have put him in a position in which he is forced to think about things that are beyond his age.

KORE-EDA: It's the theme of children being robbed of their youth. The setup of the original manga source for my last film about four sisters, *Our Little Sister* (2015), is also like this: both the oldest sister, Sachi, and the youngest sister, Suzu, were children that were denied a childhood.

I was really drawn to the manga when I first read it and realized after that it was because it was about stolen childhood.

OGAWA: There are times when you develop interest in something without really knowing why. During the funeral scene of *Our Little Sister*, when the fourth daughter (Hirose Suzu) is asked to greet the other mourners (as the chief mourner), the eldest daughter (Ayase Haruka) responds, "This is not something a child should have to do." These were meaningful words, expressing a belated effort to recover a lost childhood for the four sisters.

KORE-EDA: Yes, reading the original source text, I got a good idea of what kind of person Sachi is in that moment. It's a nice scene.

OGAWA: It really left me wondering many things. What will happen to this little boy? And should the mother really marry her boyfriend [*laughs*]?

KORE-EDA: My hope as the creator of the characters is that they are seen in that way.

OGAWA: You need unconditional love as a child. That's the very thing that allows you to spread your wings and fly.

It's Tough Becoming the Type of Person You Want to Be

MODERATOR: *After the Storm* is a family drama involving a mother (Kiki Kirin) who lives by herself in a *danchi*; her daughter (Kobayashi Satomi), who works in a confectionery shop; her son (Abe Hiroshi), a writer who won a literary award years ago but now languishes in obscurity; and her son's ex-wife (Maki Yōko) and son (Yoshizawa Taiyō).

OGAWA: The main character (Ryōta / Abe Hiroshi) is a failed writer who is, above all, bad with money. Even after the film ends, you don't get a sense that he will ever change—he's never going to win the lottery [*laughs*]. But I can't blame the character, just as I can't blame myself for thinking he will never change.

KORE-EDA: How kind [*laughs*].

OGAWA: In other words, does anyone really become who they want to be? That's also something to consider, conversely.

KORE-EDA: Are you any different?

OGAWA: Of course, I'm different in many ways [*laughs*]. I am often able to empathize with characters in films, but as a wife, mother, daughter, and writer, I saw various sides of me layered in the characters in certain scenes. Probably for that reason, I was deeply enamored with the film, as deep as the ocean, venturing with the characters to the depths before returning to the surface like a tempest from below.

KORE-EDA: This film was shot in the same *danchi* in which I was raised, so parts of me are layered within many of the characters. At times, I'm like the son or the father: I wrote myself into many of the characters. So it makes me happy to hear you say this.

OGAWA: It's not just the main characters—everyone must come to grips with the regret of not becoming what they wanted to become, even if it's not accentuated in the film. When the husband of the daughter who works in the confectionery shop comes to fix the broken glass window in his mother-in-law's apartment, he casually mentions that he always wanted to do work like this. Everyone seems to harbor these types of feelings.

KORE-EDA: That's an important line. I'm glad you noticed it.

OGAWA: There is meaning lurking in places that you may miss in your films if you're not paying attention. When I saw the face of the music teacher (Hashizume Isao), who deciphers Beethoven for the ladies in the *danchi*, reminisce about being invited to perform on television in the past, it occurred to me that even he shares these feelings.

KORE-EDA: Hashizume was brilliantly able to relay a sense of both pride and failure at the same time. I was really impressed watching him on set.

OGAWA: Did you confer with him on how to play the role before shooting?

KORE-EDA: There are actors with whom I did confer. But Hashizume got it without me having to say anything, so consulting with him seemed like it might be disrespectful.

OGAWA: It must be tricky at times to work with actors with longer careers than you.

KORE-EDA: The challenge when I first became a director was communicating with actors older than twenty or thirty. Children are tricky in a different way, as are younger staff members. Although I was the youngest on set when I first started directing, now I am the second or third oldest. With young staff members who are under thirty on set, I really need to think about the best ways to communicate with them and motivate them [*laughs*]. It can be tough.

OGAWA: Just like a middle manager at a business firm [*laughs*]. You need to appease those above and below you.

KORE-EDA: That's the position I'm in [*laughs*].

OGAWA: You'd think that directors would be able to throw their weight around [*laughs*].

KORE-EDA: There are directors who micromanage everyone—they might say that about me behind my back [*laughs*]—but I do my best to think about everyone.

Saying "Excuse Me" While Shutting the Door

KORE-EDA: You often use observers as protagonists in your stories. I also tend to position myself from the perspective of an observer. I'm not sure why—perhaps my work on documentaries has influenced the stories I write or, going back further, perhaps it's because I was often in the position of an observer as a child. It can be difficult to write stories in this way, because making your main characters observers means placing the main perspective outside of the story, but you're skilled in constructing a viewpoint that follows the story while giving the observing character a role in it.

OGAWA: When you're thrown into the world you're trying to construct, you can lose sight of the story. If you create an appropriate amount of distance from the characters and refrain from speaking, you can hear their voices. I am very conscious of creating distance. *Still Walking* (2008) was really the mother's film, wasn't it? She lost her beloved son in that way but is unable to share that pain with anyone. Even her daughter suggests that a daughter who is still alive is more useful than a dead son. But no matter how loving a relationship, no one can understand the pain of a mother who has lost a child; she must carry it alone. Even though the mother is the protagonist, the film places the son at the center of the story. It brilliantly creates distance from her in this way. Normally, I'd imagine you'd position the mother at the center.

KORE-EDA: The position of the main character is probably due to me writing the script right after my mother passed away. I lost my mother . . . so I'm writing the whole thing from the perspective of a son who lost his mother.

OGAWA: Yes, you end the film with the scene in which they visit the cemetery. Just like earlier in the film, the son pours water on the gravestone, saying, "It was hot today; you must be thirsty." If the mother from *After the Storm* died, that son would be the most broken up about it. I bet he would really lose it [*laughs*].

KORE-EDA: Do you think it'd hit him at that point [*laughs*]? I wonder [*laughs*].

OGAWA: Your films do not tell you to pay attention or warn you that you should pay attention. There are no tricks to force you to notice something.

KORE-EDA: It would be presumptuous of me as the creator to tell the viewer that they need to do something.

OGAWA: It's like if you were to judge a character that you yourself created.

KORE-EDA: Exactly. Your book, *The Function of Narrative* [*Monogatari no yakuwari*, 2007], was helpful in this regard; I found your statement reassuring that writers do not create things but unearth things that already exist in the story. When making *Nobody Knows*, I was asked repeatedly why I didn't judge the mother. Why not take responsibility in the world of the work? The mother should have either fallen on hard times or realized her mistakes and reformed her ways. It might be my film, but I am not its god and have no intention of passing judgment. So your statement in *The Function of Narrative* about only being able to truly write a story once you humbly accept that the story exists without your own intervention was convincing.

OGAWA: As observers, we're not in the position to judge anyone. We are allowed to observe for a while and then go our way. We say "excuse me" while shutting the door.

KORE-EDA: That's a good way of putting it [*laughs*].

OGAWA: Documentaries must work like this, too, with a bunch of people who aren't supposed to be there hanging around.

KORE-EDA: Exactly. Not forgetting that you are an imposition is important in documentary filmmaking. In making this film, I worked with the same cinematographer, Yamazaki Yutaka, from my documentary filmmaking days. He would let me know whether camera positions were an intrusion. It's about finding positions that don't interfere with daily life.

The Family That Is No Longer There

OGAWA: *After the Storm* closely depicted the reality of living in a *danchi*, down to the details—the things that the mother couldn't bring herself to part with, the image of her working in the kitchen with her back to us. All these things seemed part of the place rather than things created for the film.

KORE-EDA: Thank you very much. It's based on my life, so I really wanted to get it right.

OGAWA: The mother and daughter chat unguardedly while cooking and writing postcards. It really shows the way struggles of the past become fodder for laughs.

KORE-EDA: I was trying to suggest that this is not a sad film.

OGAWA: But [the mother] will always worry about her son like he is ten years old, no matter how old he gets.

KORE-EDA: I really like the part in your story "Bluffman's Burial" ["Burafuman no maisō," 2004] in which they buy the old pictures of family and decorate their house with them. And the store owner tells them to treasure the pictures.

OGAWA: Thank you. I'm beginning to forget half the things I've written [*laughs*].

KORE-EDA: I liked the idea of hanging pictures of a family that you don't even know. I don't know why, but it made a lasting impression on me.

OGAWA: Perhaps it's better not to give a logical explanation why we take an interest in certain things, why we like them.

KORE-EDA: The moment you try to put it into words, it seems fake. *The Housekeeper and the Professor*, "Bluffman's Burial," and "Kotori" are all like this. You often try to capture things that are no longer there.

OGAWA: That might be too bold of a statement, but novels capture people who were once here but are no longer. The novel came about as a way of reviving things that were lost to language. No matter who writes them, novels do not function from a perspective of being able to see the future. They don't try to predict what will happen to characters but rather seek to trace their footsteps.

KORE-EDA: I think I would like that aspect of it.

OGAWA: The family in the film is shown in this way, but at this point they have already lost something. Speaking of which, Kiki Kirin is always working in the film. But that is how mothers are, right? Always working.

KORE-EDA: The way Kiki Kirin talks while laying out the bedding and the pajamas was really on point. At some point you'd want to stop her, but she kept moving.

OGAWA: Kiki Kirin realizes that her son might be bad with money, but he has a talent that not many other people have. And on the night of the storm, she reminds her grandson that love still exists in their broken family—though it seems like she is trying to convince herself. In the scene in which the mother said that she has never loved anyone with a love deeper than the ocean while listening to Teresa Teng's song, I wanted to hit my desk, stand up, and yell, "That's not true [*laughs*]!"

KORE-EDA: Kiki Kirin asked if her lines might be too preachy, thinking about all aspects of her performance. Even on set she questioned the placement of props—where would someone living alone leave their radio?—and made sure that she could open the refrigerator door without looking. She scrutinized the set just like a new actor to make it fit her body. After living in the apartment for so many decades, her body would know the space.

OGAWA: All this unseen calculation and preparation is amazing. The morning after the storm, Kiki Kirin sees the three family members off from the veranda. If you look beyond the futon lined up neatly on the veranda, there are stories that are deeper than the ocean, and I had the pleasure of seeing one of them.

"Rirī Furankī, the Father of the Family, Osamu, Director Kore-eda Hirokazu Takes a Step into New Territory after Ten Years," by Todoroki Yukio et al.

This interview is a short discussion between Kore-eda and one of his actors, Rirī Furankī, who plays the father of the Shibata family in *Shoplifters*. The discussion was moderated by Japanese film critic Todoroki Yukio. Rirī Furankī has appeared in four of Kore-eda's films, playing supporting roles in *Like Father, Like Son*; *Our Little Sister*; and *After the Storm* and a more central role in *Shoplifters*. The interview was given a short time after the release of *Shoplifters*, providing Kore-eda and Rirī little time to process the film before reacting to it. Unlike other interviews, which deal more with the formal style and thematic content of Kore-eda's films, this interview gets into the social consciousness of films such as *Nobody Knows* and *Shoplifters*.

MODERATOR: The film that originally took the name "Read Out Loud" as its working title eventually became *Shoplifters*. This is Kore-eda's latest film offering. This discussion between Kore-eda and Riri Furanki, the main character in the story, took place right after the completion of the film before the start of the seventy-first Cannes Film Festival in May and even before the press conference announcing its completion on April 25. Feeling their way through the conversation, they shared some insights into the meaning of the film.

A Film Filled with Anger

RIRI: I haven't quite figured out this film yet.

KORE-EDA: Me neither. I'm still too close to it. At any rate, I felt like it was a "bold" film after watching it—something bold captured on film.

RIRI: I was shocked when I saw the rush print. It had changed so much from the original plot and screenplay. I cried when I first read the screenplay; its lyricism touched me deeply. However, during shooting, it felt more like a warm family drama, if not a comedy. Comparing these early impressions with the final product, it was just like watching a documentary of a family struggling to survive.

KORE-EDA: My sound person, Hosono Harumi, watched the film and asked if it was alright not to add music because it seemed more like a documentary. I surely didn't set out to make a documentary, but the production of the film resembled the documentary filmmaking process. In other words, I was constantly revising the screenplay based on the moments when motifs that even I did not anticipate would emerge as we shot and edited the film. The film is completely fictional, but its overall feel is a product of my documentary-like approach.

MODERATOR: The real-life domestic fraud incidents in Japan of people stealing the pensions of their deceased parents inspired your imagination as a writer. [You mentioned in a press conference that] "when I heard the family members make excuses for crimes by saying that they couldn't accept that their loved one had died, I wanted to imagine the full story behind these statements" (quoted from *Press Sit* [Q&A]). You thought they could be lying, so you sketched a family that is connected only by crime. The film begins with the father, Shibata Osamu (played by Rirī), and son, Shōta (Jyō Kairi), teaming up on one of their shoplifting jobs and then cuts to them walking home on the cold winter night as Osamu, who can't bring himself to leave behind a little girl (Sasaki Miyu) they find shivering in the cold in the slums of a high-rise apartment, takes her home with them. At the press conference, you said that "anger was the emotion at the center of making this film."

RIRĪ: Kore-eda always seems angry about something.

KORE-EDA: Yes, about various things, surprisingly [*laughs*]. Sorting through the emotions behind this film is tricky, but if I had to choose one at the basis of the film, it was anger. More specifically, I needed to critique the indifferent coverage of the family in these types of incidents, coverage that does not attempt to flesh out the subjects but rather stands aside and apathetically watches the deterioration of the family. *Nobody Knows* (2014) was like this too—I channeled the perspective inspired by my malaise toward society through my anger. That's why the film seems "bold" to me.

RIRĪ: Perhaps it's because children like Shōta are the main characters in the film, and when you feature children in your films, social problems are shown in greater relief because the film takes on the perspective of these most vulnerable members of society. I really like this about your films. Your work is journalistic by nature, mingled with the perspective of a filmmaker. These two aspects combine to create the sense of anger in your films.

KORE-EDA: Thank you.

RIRĪ: However, there are surely tone-deaf critics who condemn the film for supporting shoplifting in this day and age.

KORE-EDA: Yes, there surely are.

RIRĪ: Certainly, from a legal standpoint, [the family in *Shoplifters*] is doing something wrong, and we shouldn't advocate for it, but they are also surprisingly good people. Playing Shibata Osamu and spending time in that family helped me reconsider the source of human happiness and realize that we don't live in a black-and-white world.

KORE-EDA: Yes, I agree. Certainly, they have a lot of problems, but they're also happy together. Can you really question their smiles? I wonder . . .

RIRĪ: Your anger in this film is directed toward something that often upsets me too, how mass and online media make simple judgments about good and evil that only scratch the surface of events and then attack and demolish those responsible without going any further. The world is increasingly becoming a place in which reasons and circumstances hidden beneath the surface are ignored. Amid all this, your approach is refreshing. There are often underlying reasons for committing "crimes" that we should be aware of before passing judgment.

The Bright Stars in the Kore-eda Club

MODERATOR: Rirī, you have been in four Kore-eda films, including this one [*Shoplifters*]; *Like Father, Like Son*; *Our Little Sister*; and *After the Storm*—second most to Kiki Kirin, who plays the part of the grandmother. This shows how much Kore-eda must trust you as an actor. Osamu's wife, Nobuyo, who is played by Andō Sakura, and Nobuyo's sister, Aki, who works at the sex club, played by Matsuoka Mayu, are making their first appearances as part of the Kore-eda Club. Their performances are outstanding, but you, Rirī, are really the center of the film.

RIRĪ: I think the thing that surprised me the most when we started shooting was the rawness of Sakura's and Mayu's performances. I was inspired by their unvarnished approach, which lacked any vanity. Needless to say, Kirin was the same. The way she would take out her dentures and eat oranges in an unpleasant way was uncompromising.

KORE-EDA: When I had her eat *zenzai* at the confectionery shop, I thought, "Is she sucking on the mochi [*laughs*]?"

RIRĪ: With no teeth, she couldn't chew the mochi, so she put it on Aki's plate. What amazing acting [*laughs*]! An actor's physiology really comes into play. Something that concerned me a little was that my voice didn't match the role I was playing. Even Kirin said my voice sounded too intellectual for the father of a shoplifting family. But changing too much seemed calculating.

KORE-EDA: I love your voice, so it really wasn't a problem, but the nuance at the end of your sentences was a little too much in a few places. There is a bit of flatness at the end of your lines.

RIRĪ: Really!?!

KORE-EDA: But more than that, what I was reminded of was not just the quality of your performance but also how your fine motor skills are on the level of a professional athlete. You are familiar with how your body looks on film and what happens when you move. It's like when a professional soccer player can see themselves from a third-person perspective as they dribble. You have that sense, don't you?

RIRĪ: That's the first time anyone has told me that. I rarely receive compliments from you, but I can think of two instances. The first was when you said I could put my pants on really quickly. And the second was unrelated to my performance, but it was when you complimented the way I could crouch with my heels touching the ground.

This Is Not the End

MODERATOR: In the film, the thing that quietly encourages Shōta as he skips out on middle school is the story "Swimmy," which is published in his textbook. Created by the American picture-book artist Leo Lionni, who is originally from the Netherlands, "Swimmy" is the tale of one black fish in a school of red fish. The Japanese translation is by the poet Tanikawa Shuntarō. It seems like a poetic tale like the one in "Swimmy" emerges about this family, who is held together by crime and who has been abandoned by society.

KORE-EDA: In the original screenplay, Shōta overtakes his father at the end of the story, but what this means is something that I realized only while shooting. In this plot configuration, there are parts of the film, though rare, that reflect my life, and within Shōta, the image of Osamu as a father figure is shattered. Osamu's dysfunction stimulates Shōta's growth. That's the reason Osamu suffered in the past, and now, as a parent, Osamu has a hard time accepting the situation. Lately, I get the feeling that this is what it means to be a father.

RIRĪ: You told me that Osamu is a good-for-nothing character. He doesn't grow up in the end. But because he doesn't change, everyone around him is able to move on. Other than Osamu, everyone grows.

KORE-EDA: About Osamu's wife, Nobuyo, Osamu's irresponsible adoption of the little girl brings out her motherly instincts. I wanted to show how people change through the accumulation of these kinds of acts, even if they don't recognize it themselves.

RIRĪ: The scene in which the family all go to the beach during the summer was also memorable. All there was at that point in the shooting was plot.

KORE-EDA: By shooting this scene first, I was able to envision a lot of the story, and this allowed me to write the whole film. On set, Kirin abruptly suggested that she say to Nobuyo, "If one looks closely enough, you're beautiful." Shooting the scene, I realized that it was a moment in which Nobuyo was seen from a transcendent perspective. At that point in the story, Kirin was able to see everything. It's that kind of story.

RIRĪ: It's also the scene in which Kirin reveals the girlish side of the grandmother role. I really like that scene. But when I asked you after we shot it, you said you just wanted to bring the cast to scout out locations.

KORE-EDA: Right. It happened by chance.

RIRĪ: When we all stood together in the ocean, it seemed like the "poor version" of *Our Little Sister*. Mayu thought that was a perfect description when I told her about it, but she asked me not to mention it. Because, she cried, "I really wanted to be in *Our Little Sister* [*laughs*]!"

KORE-EDA: You mentioned that this film is a "poor version" of *Our Little Sister*. . . . [C]ome to think of it, the half-sister of the three girls in *Our Little Sister* moves in. As with *Shoplifters*, domestic relationships change when a young girl joins the family. I wouldn't call *Shoplifters* the culmination of my career, but it really reflects the things that I have been thinking about over the last ten years.

RIRĪ: Even if you suppress your natural instincts as a writer or film-maker, they eventually come out. I really think *Shoplifters* combines everything that is important to your work up until now while also constituting a step into new territory.

Feature Films

Maboroshi no hikari (*Maborosi*, 1995)
Japan
Production company: TV Man Union
Producer: Gōzu Naoe
Writer (novel): Miyamoto Teru
Screenplay: Ogita Yoshihisa
Cinematographer: Nakabori Masao
Editor: Ōshima Tomoyo
Cast: Esumi Makiko, Naitō Takashi, Asano Tadanobu
Color
110 min.

Wandāfuru raifu (*After Life*, 1998)
Japan
Production company: TV Man Union, Engine Film, Sputnik Productions
Producer: Akieda Masayuki
Writer: Kore-eda Hirokazu
Cinematographers: Sukita Masayoshi, Yamazaki Yutaka
Editor: Kore-eda Hirokazu
Cast: Arata, Oda Erika, Terajima Susumu
Color
119 min.

Disutansu (*Distance*, 2001)
Japan
Production company: Distance Project Team, TV Man Union, Engine Film,
    CineRocket
Producer: Akieda Masayuki
Writer: Kore-eda Hirokazu
Cinematographer: Yamazaki Yutaka

Editor: Kore-eda Hirokazu
Cast: Arata, Iseya Yūsuke, Terajima Susumu, Asano Tadanobu
Color
132 min.

Dare mo shiranai (*Nobody Knows*, 2004)
Japan
Production company: TV Man Union, Bandai Visual, Engine Film, Cine Qua Non
Producer: Kore-eda Hirokazu
Writer: Kore-eda Hirokazu
Cinematographer: Yamazaki Yutaka
Editor: Kore-eda Hirokazu
Cast: Yagira Yūya, Kitaura Ayu, Kimura Hiei, You
Color
141 min.

Hana yori mo naho (*Hana: The Tale of the Reluctant Samurai*, 2006)
Japan
Production company: Shōchiku, Engine Film, TV Man Union, Bandai Visual,
    Eisei Gekijo
Producer: Enoki Nozomi
Writer: Kore-eda Hirokazu
Cinematographer: Yamazaki Yutaka
Editor: Kore-eda Hirokazu
Cast: Okada Jun'ichi, Miyazawa Rie, Arata
Color
127 min.

Aruitemo aruitemo (*Still Walking*, 2008)
Japan
Production company: Engine Film, Bandai Visual, TV Man Union, Eisei Gekijo,
    Cine Qua Non
Producer: Hisamatsu Takeo
Writer: Kore-eda Hirokazu
Cinematographer: Yamazaki Yutaka
Editor: Kore-eda Hirokazu
Cast: Abe Hiroshi, Natsukawa Yui, You, Kiki Kirin
Color
114 min.

Daijōbu de aru yōni: Cocco owaranai tabi (*So It's Alright: Cocco's Endless
    Journey*, 2008)
Japan
Production company: TV Man Union

Producer: Kore-eda Hirokazu
Cinematographer: Yamazaki Yutaka
Editor: Kore-eda Hirokazu
Cast: Cocco
Color
107 min.

Kūki ningyō (*Air Doll*, 2009)
Japan
Production company: Engine Film, TV Man Union, Bandai Visual, Eisei Gekijo
Producer: Kore-eda Hirokazu
Writer (manga): Gōda Yoshiie
Screenplay: Kore-eda Hirokazu
Cinematographer: Ping Bin Lee
Editor: Kore-eda Hirokazu
Cast: Bae Doona, Arata, Itao Itsuji
Color
125 min.

Kiseki (*I Wish*, 2011)
Japan
Production company: Shirogumi Inc., GAGA, Bandai Visual
Producer: Koike Kentarō
Writer: Kore-eda Hirokazu
Cinematographer: Yamazaki Yutaka
Editor: Kore-eda Hirokazu
Cast: Nagasawa Masami, Odagiri Jō, Abe Hiroshi, Kiki Kirin, Natsukawa Yui
Color
128 min.

Soshite chichi ni naru (*Like Father, Like Son*, 2013)
Japan
Production company: Amuse, Fuji Television, GAGA, Bunbuku
Producer: Harada Chiaki
Screenplay: Kore-eda Hirokazu
Cinematographer: Takimoto Mikiya
Editor: Kore-eda Hirokazu
Cast: Fukuyama Masaharu, Ono Machiko, Maki Yōko, Rirī Furankī
Color
121 min.

Umimachi diary (*Our Little Sister*, 2015)
Japan
Production company: Fuji Television, Toho, GAGA, Bunbuku, TV Man Union

Producer: Ichikawa Minami
Writer (manga): Yoshida Akimi
Screenplay: Kore-eda Hirokazu
Cinematographer: Takimoto Mikiya
Editor: Kore-eda Hirokazu
Cast: Ayase Haruka, Nagasawa Masami, Kaho, Hirose Suzu
Color
127 min.

Umi yori mo mada fukaku (*After the Storm*, 2016)
Japan
Production company: Aoi Promotion, Bandai Visual, Fuji Television, GAGA
Producer: Fujiwara Tsugihiko
Writer: Kore-eda Hirokazu
Cinematographer: Yamazaki Yutaka
Editor: Kore-eda Hirokazu
Cast: Abe Hiroshi, Maki Yōko, Kobayashi Satomi, Rirī Furankī
Color
118 min.

Sandome no satsujin (*The Third Murder*, 2017)
Japan
Production company: Amuse, Fuji 1G Laboratory for Movies, Fuji Television,
    GAGA
Producer: Harada Chiaki
Writer: Kore-eda Hirokazu
Cinematographer: Takimoto Mikiya
Editor: Kore-eda Hirokazu
Cast: Fukuyama Masaharu, Yakusho Kōji, Mitsushima Shinnosuke
Color
124 min.

Manbiki kazoku (*Shoplifters*, 2018)
Japan
Production company: AOI Promotion, Fuji Television, GAGA
Producer: Ishihara Takashi
Writer: Kore-eda Hirokazu
Cinematographer: Kondō Ryūto
Editor: Kore-eda Hirokazu
Cast: Rirī Furankī, Andō Sakura, Kiki Kirin
Color
121 min.

La vérité / The Truth / Shinjitsu (2019)
France, Japan, Switzerland
Production company: 3B Productions, Bunbuku, M1 Films, France3 Cinema
Producer: Muriel Merlin
Writer (film in a film based on a short story by): Ken Liu
Screenplay: Kore-eda Hirokazu
Cinematographer: Eric Gautier
Editor: Kore-eda Hirokazu
Cast: Catherine Deneuve, Juliette Binoche, Ethan Hawke
Color
106 min.

Beurokeo (*Broker*, 2022)
South Korea, Japan
Production company: Zip Cinema
Producer: Eugene Lee
Writer: Kore-eda Hirokazu
Cast: Bae Doona, Song Kang-ho, Lee Ji-eun
Color
129 min.

Television Documentaries

Mō hitotsu no kyōiku—Ina shōgakkō harugumi no kiroku (*Lessons from a Calf—
Record at the Spring Class at Ina Elementary School*, 1991)
Japan
Broadcast: Fuji TV *Nonfix*
Production company: TV Man Union
Producer: Kore-eda Hirokazu
Writer: Kore-eda Hirokazu
Cinematographer: Kore-eda Hirokazu
Editor: Kore-eda Hirokazu
Color
47 min.

Shikashi . . . fukushi kirisute no jidai ni (*However . . . in the Time of Govern-
ment Aid Cuts*, 1991)
Japan
Broadcast: Fuji TV *Nonfix*
Production company: TV Man Union
Producer: Kore-eda Hirokazu
Writer: Kore-eda Hirokazu

Cinematographer: Itō Shinji
Editor: Nakamura Yukihiro
Cast: Morimoto Reo, Yamanouchi Toyonori, Kitagawa Ishimatsu
Color
47 min.

Kōgai wa doko e itta (*Where Has Pollution Gone*, 1992)
Japan
Broadcast: Fuji TV *Nonfix*
Production company: TV Man Union
Color
47 min.

Nihonjin ni naritakatta (*I Wanted to Be Japanese*, 1992)
Japan
Broadcast: Fuji TV *Nonfix*
Production company: TV Man Union
Color
47 min.

Hō Shiao-shin to Edowa-do Yan (*Hou Hsiao-hsien and Edward Yang*, 1993)
Japan
Broadcast: Fuji TV *Nonfix*
Production company: TV Man Union
Color
47 min.
A program on the work of Taiwanese directors Hou Hsiao-hsien and Edward
Yang.

AIDS to ikiru hito—Hirata Yutaka san wa kataru (*This Is How I'm Living with
AIDS—Hirata Yutaka Recounts*, 1993)
Japan
Production company: TV Man Union
Color
24 min.

Shinshō sukecchi, sorezore no Miyazawa Kenji (*Soul Sketches, Various Miyazawa
Kenjis*, 1993)
Japan
Broadcast: TV Tokyo
Color
45 min.
A profile of Japanese writer Miyazawa Kenji.

Kare no inai hachigatsu ga (*August without Him*, 1994)
Japan
Broadcast: Fuji TV *Nonfix* special
Production company: TV Man Union
Color
78 min.

Kioku ga ushinawareta toki (*Without Memory*, 1996)
Japan
Broadcast: NHK
Production company: TV Man Union, NHK
Producer: Hayashi Katsuhiko
Cinematographer: Honda Shigeru
Editor: Kore-eda Hirokazu
Cast: Sekine Hiroshi, Sekine Miwa
Color
84 min.

Aruku yōna hayasa de (*Moving at a Walking Pace*, 2003)
Japan
Broadcast: Nihon TV

Shiriizu kenpō, dai kyūjyō, sensō hōki 'bōkyaku' (*The Constitution Series: Article
    9—Renouncing War*, 2005)
Japan
Broadcast: Fuji TV *Nonfix*
Production company: TV Man Union
Color
47 min.
A program on attempts to revise Article 9 of the Japanese Constitution.

Watashi ga kodomo datta koro—Tanikawa Shuntarō hen (*When I Was a Child:
    The Works of Tanikawa Shuntarō*, 2007)
Japan
Broadcast: NHK *High Vision*
Color
A program on one of the most widely read Japanese poets.

Ano toki datta kamoshirenai: Terebi ni totte 'watashi' to wa nani ka (*It Could
    Have Been That Time: What "I" Mean to TV*, 2008)
Japan
Broadcast: TBS/BS
Color

Warui no wa minna Hagimoto Kin'ichi de aru (*The Bad Ones Are All Hagimoto Kin'ichi*, 2010)
Japan
Broadcast: Fuji TV
Color
A program on the Japanese comedian Hagimoto Kin'ichi.

Fukushima kara no messēji (*A Message from Fukushima*, 2012)
Japan
Color
A program on the 2011 Tōhoku earthquake and tsunami.
16 min.

Kyō no, akinai (*Today's Business*, 2015)
Japan
Broadcast: TBS
A program that documents various businesses that deal in not only physical goods such as food and clothes but also intangible things such as emotion, time, and space.

Ishibumi . . . wasurenai. Anatatachi no koto wo . . . (*I Will Never Forget You, Ishibumi*, 2015)
Japan
Broadcast: Nihon TV
Production company: Documentary Japan
Producer: Hashimoto Yoshiko
Writer (original story): Usukida Jun'ichirō
Teleplay: Matsuyama Zenzō
Cinematographers: Kōno Hiroki, Suzuki Katsuhiko, Yamazaki Yutaka
Cast: Ayase Haruka, Ikegami Akira
Color
85 min.
A television program about the atomic bombing of Hiroshima, Japan.

Television Dramas

Ayashiki bungo kaidan (*Kaidan Horror Classics*, season 1, episode 4, "Dead Son," 2010)
Japan
Production company: TV Man Union
Producer: Hamano Takahiro
Writer (novel): Murō Saisei
Casting director: Tabata Toshie

Cast: Kase Ryō, Nakamura Yuri
Color
75 min.

Going My Home (season 1, episodes 1, 2, 8, 9, 10, 2012)
Japan
Production company: TV Man Union
Producers: Kazuhisa Andō
Writer: Kore-eda Hirokazu (five episodes)
Editor: Kore-eda Hirokazu (four episodes)
Cast: Aoi Tatsumi, Abe Hiroshi, Yamaguchi Tomoko, Miyazaki Aoi
Color
51 min.
A ten-part television series that follows the story of Tsuboi Ryōta, a producer
for a commercial production company, and his family.

Arimura Kasumi no satsukyū (*Arimura Kasumi's Holidays*, one episode, "A Day
Off for Kasumi Arimura," 2020)
Japan
Production company: WOWOW
Teleplay: Higa Sakura, Sunada Mami
Cast: Arimura Kasumi
Color
85 min.
A miniseries about the fictionalized life of Japanese actress Arimura Kasumi.

Maiko-san chi no makanai-san (*The Makanai: Cooking for the Maiko House,*
2023)
Japan (Netflix, eight episodes)
Production company: Bunbuku
Teleplay: Koyama Aiko
Cast: Matsuoka Mayu, Hashimoto Ai, Mori Nana
Color

Althusser, Louis. *On the Reproduction of Capitalism: Ideology and Ideological State Apparatuses*. New York: Verso, 2014.

Arai Toshinori. "Kore-eda Hirokazu: Miageru to—'Shinjitsu' nanoka kan yon jyūsan nichi no Monogatari" [Kore-eda Hirokazu: On second consideration—"The Truth," a forty-three-day story in seven days]. *Switch* 11.37 (2019): 12–23.

Archibald, David. "Team Loach and Sixteen Films: Authorship, Collaboration, Leadership (and Football)." *Contemporary Cinema and Neoliberal Ideology*. Ed. Ewa Mazierska and Lars Kristensen. London: Taylor & Francis Group, 2017. 25–41.

Bingham, Adam. *Contemporary Japanese Cinema Since Hana-bi*. Edinburgh: Edinburgh UP, 2015.

Binoche, Juliette, and Kore-eda Hirokazu. "Jurietto Binoshu: Hikizan ga yori yoi tashizan ni" [Juliette Binoche: Addition by subtraction]. *Sekai to ima wo kangaeru: Kore-eda Hirokazu taidanshū 1* [Thinking about the world now: Conversations with Kore-eda Hirokazu, part 1]. Ed. Kore-eda Hirokazu. Tokyo: PHP, 2016. 151–87.

Bradshaw, Peter. "Hirokazu Kore-eda: 'They Compare Me to Ozu. But I'm More Like Ken Loach.'" *Guardian* 21 May 2015.

Brennan, Teresa. *The Transmission of Affect*. Ithaca, NY: Cornell UP, 2004.

Brenner, Neil, and Nik Theodore. "Cities and the Geographies of 'Actually Existing Neoliberalism.'" *Spaces of Neoliberalism: Urban Restructuring in North America and Western Europe*. Ed. Neil Brenner and Nik Theodore. Oxford: Blackwell, 2002. 2–32.

Brown, Wendy. "Neo-liberalism and the End of Liberal Democracy." *Theory & Event* 7.1 (2003). https://muse.jhu.edu/article/48659.

Bruno, Giuliana. *Atlas of Emotion: Journeys in Art, Architecture, and Film*. New York: Verso, 2002.

Cardullo, Bert. "Life and Nothing But." *Hudson Review* 51.2 (1998): 409–16.

Casey, Edward. *The Fate of Place: A Philosophical History*. Berkeley: U of California P, 1997.

Cercel, Christian. "Whither Politics, Whither Memory?" *Modern Languages Open* 1 (2020). http://doi.org/10.3828/mlo.voio.334.

Certeau, Michel de. *The Practice of Everyday Life*. Berkeley: U of California P, 1980.

Chang, Kee. "Q&A with Hirokazu Kore-eda." *Anthem Magazine* 17 Nov. 2018. http://anthemmagazine.com/qa-with-hirokazu-kore-eda/.

Condry, Ian. *The Soul of Anime*. Durham, NC: Duke UP, 2013.

Cooper, Anna. "Neoliberal Theory and Film Studies." *New Review of Film and Television Studies* 17.3 (2019): 265–77. https://doi.org/10.1080/17400309 .2019.1622877.

Deleuze, Gilles. *Cinema 2: The Time Image*. Trans. H. Tomlinson and R. Galeta. London: Athlone Press, 1989.

Deleuze, Gilles, and Félix Guattari. *Anti-Oedipus: Capitalism and Schizophrenia*. Vol. 1. Trans. Robert Hurley, Mark Seem, and Helen R. Lane. London: Athlone, 1984.

———. *A Thousand Plateaus: Capitalism and Schizophrenia*. Vol. 2. Trans. Brian Massumi. London: Athlone, 1988.

———. *What Is Philosophy?* London: Verso Books, 1994.

Desser, David. "*After Life*: History, Memory, Trauma and the Transcendent." *Film Criticism* 35.2/3 (2011): 46–65.

———. "The Imagination of the Transcendent: Kore-eda Hirokazu's *Maborosi* (1995)." *Japanese Cinema: Texts and Contexts*. Ed. Julian Stringer and Alastair Phillips. London: Routledge, 2007. 273–78.

Dorman, Andrew. *Paradoxical Japaneseness: Cultural Representations in 21st Century Japanese Cinema*. London: Palgrave, 2016.

Ehrlich, Linda C. *The Films of Kore-eda Hirokazu: An Elemental Cinema*. New York: Palgrave, 2019.

Elliot, Jane, and Gillian Harkins. "Introduction: Genres of Neoliberalism." *Social Text* 31.2 (Summer 2013 [115]): 1–17.

Ellis, Jonathan. "Review of *After Life*." *Film Quarterly* 57.1 (Fall 2003): 32–37.

Feinsod, Mark, and Hirokazu Kore-eda. "A Conversation with 'Maborosi' Director, Hirokazu Kore-Eda—Part 1." *Indiewire* 5 Sept. 1996. https://www .indiewire.com/1996/09/a-conversation-with-maborosi-director-hirokazu -kore-eda-part-i-83630/.

Foucault, Michel. *The History of Sexuality, Volume 1: An Introduction*. Trans. Robert Hurley. New York: Vintage, 1990.

Fukuoka Shin'ichi and Kore-eda Hirokazu. "Sono shunkan no, zengo ni sonzai suru mono" [In that instant, the things right behind you]. *Sekai to ima wo kangaeru: Kore-eda Hirokazu taidanshū 3* [Thinking about the world now: Conversations with Kore-eda Hirokazu, part 3]. Ed. Kore-eda Hirokazu. Tokyo: PHP, 2016. 189–220.

Fukuyama Masaharu and Kore-eda Hirokazu. "Nidome no koraboreshion de, mezashita mono" [Things we are looking forward to in a second collaboration]. *Kinema Junpō* 1756 (Sept. 2017): 22–27.

Gerow, Aaron, and Kore-eda Hirokazu. "Documentarists of Japan #12: Kore-eda Hirokazu." *Yamagata International Documentary Film Festival*. https://www.yidff.jp/docbox/13/box13-1-e.html. Accessed 11 Feb. 2021.

Gill, Tom. "When Pillars Evaporate: Structuring Masculinity on the Japanese Margins." *Men and Masculinities in Contemporary Japan: Dislocating the Salaryman Doxa*. Ed. James E. Roberson and Nobue Suzuki. New York: Routledge Curzon, 2003. 144–61.

Gordon, Andrew. "Making Sense of the Lost Decades: Workplaces and Schools, Men and Women, Young and Old, Rich and Poor." *Examining Japan's Lost Decades*. Ed. Yoichi Funabashi and Barak Kushner. New York: Routledge, 2015. 77–100.

Halle, Randall. "Toward a Phenomenology of Emotion in Film: Michael Brynntrup and the Face of Gay Shame." *Emotionality*. German issue of *MLN* 124.3 (Apr. 2009): 683–707.

Hase Masato. "Sōmei na sakka, Kore-eda Hirokazu" [Wise writer, Kore-eda Hirokazu]. *Kore-eda Hirokazu: Mata koko kara hajimaru* [Kore-eda Hirokazu: Starting from this point again]. Ed. Sen Misa. Tokyo: Kawade, 2017. 124–32.

Hayashi, Sharon. "The Rise of Collectives and the Redefinition of Labor, Life, and Representation in Neoliberal Japan." *Neoliberalism and Global Cinema: Capital, Culture, and Marxist Critique*. Ed. Jyotsna Kapur and Keith B. Wagner. New York: Taylor & Francis Group, 2011. 180–96.

Higuchi Naofumi. "Kore-eda waurudo no kekkai ga hirogatta junsaku" [A masterpiece that expands Kore-eda Land]. *Kinema Junpō* 1756 (Sept. 2017): 30–31.

———. "Narushishizumu wo nukete 'mono no aware'" ["Mono no aware" without narcissism]. *Kinema Junpō* 1511 (July 2008): 54–55.

Hiltunen, Kaisa. "Closeness in Film Experience: At the Intersection of Cinematic and Human Skin." *Corpus: The Bodily Turn—Gesture, Gender and Sensation of the Art* 12 Dec. 2011. http://www.corpus-aesthetics.net/journal.php.

Hokazono Yuriko and Kore-eda Hirokazu. "Ronguitabyu—Kore-eda Hirokazu—eiga kantoku" [Interview with film director Kore-eda Hirokazu]. *Associe*, 1 July 2008, 104–11.

Hori Kaori and Kore-eda Hirokazu. "Kore-eda Hirokazu: Kotoba wo koete bijon wo kyōyū suru" [Kore-eda Hirokazu: Sharing a vision beyond words]. *Switch* 11.37 (2019): 24–35.

Hosoda Mamoru and Kore-eda Hirokazu. "Eiga wo tsukuru koto wa kōen wo tsukuru yōna mono" [Making a film is like making a public park]. Kore-eda, *Sekai to ima wo kangaeru 3* 10–44.

Iijima Nami and Kawauchi Rinko. "Kore-eda gumi de shigoto wo suru to iu koto" [Working in the Kore-eda Club]. Sen, *Kore-eda Hirokazu* 138–57.

Ishii-Kuntz, Masako. "Balancing Fatherhood and Work: Emergence of Diverse Masculinities in Japan." Roberson and Suzuki, *Men and Masculinities* 198–216.

Jacoby, Alexander. "Why Nobody Knows: Family and Society in Modern Japan." *Film Criticism* 35.2/3 (2011): 66–83.

Jenner, Mareike. *Netflix and the Reinvention of Television*. London: Palgrave Macmillan, 2018.

Jia Zhangke and Kore-eda Hirokazu. "Independento eiga no chihei: Riarizumu to shijō de egakareru hitobito no itonami" [Independent film on the ground level: Depicting human activity with realism and poetry]. Kore-eda, *Sekai to ima wo kangaeru 1* 9–34.

Jonze, Spike, and Kore-eda Hirokazu. "Hihyō no me mochitsuzukeru tame ni" [Keeping a critical eye]. Kore-eda, *Sekai to ima wo kangaeru 1* 35–54.

Kan Sanjun and Kore-eda Hirokazu. *Switch intabyu—tatsujin tatsu: Kore-eda Hirokazu × Kan Sanjun* [*Switch* interview—expert and expert: Kore-eda Hirokazu and Kan Sanjun]. Tokyo: NHK, 2014.

Kanazawa Makoto and Kore-eda Hirokazu. "Kore-eda Hirokazu 'kantoku' intabyu (sakuhin tokushū 'aruite mo, aruite mo')" [Kore-eda Hirokazu: Director interview (featured work *Still Walking*)]. *Kinema Junpō* 1511 (July 2008): 50–53.

Kawakami Hiromi and Kore-eda Hirokazu. "'Usobanshi' ga umareru shunkan" [The moment a "fiction" is born]. *Sekai to ima wo kangaeru: Kore-eda Hirokazu taidanshū 2* [Thinking about the world now: Conversations with Kore-eda Hirokazu, part 2]. Ed. Kore-eda Hirokazu. Tokyo: PHP, 2016. 9–25.

Kingston, Jeff. *Contemporary Japan: History, Politics, and Social Change Since the 1980s*. Hoboken, NJ: Wiley-Blackwell, 2013.

Kishida Kururi and Kore-eda Hirokazu. "Sakuhin wo futoku suru tame no 'mae muki no dakyō'" [A "constructive compromise" to thicken the work]. Kore-eda, *Sekai to ima wo kangaeru 2* 139–51.

Konno Tsutomu and Kore-eda Hirokazu. "Itami Jūzō to terebi" [Itami Jūzō and television]. Sen, *Kore-eda Hirokazu* 76–103.

Kore-eda Hirokazu. *Aruku yōna hayasa de* [Moving at a walking pace]. Tokyo: Ichio Otsuka, 2013.

———. "Chichi no shakkin" [My father's debts]. Kore-eda, *Sekai to ima wo kangaeru 3* 383–92.

———. "Dokyumentari—to fikushion no sōgo noriire: Kore-eda Hirokazu" [On the reciprocity between documentary and fiction: Kore-eda Hirokazu]. *Kōkoku Hihyō* 275 (Oct. 2003): 80–89.

———. "Eiga kantoku Kore-eda Hirokazu: Intabyu" [Interview: Film director Kore-eda Hirokazu]. *Shūkan Tōyō Keizai* 6335 (July 2011): 118–19.

———. "Kore-eda Hirokazu wo tsukutta sakuhin 66" [The 66 films that made Kore-eda Hirokazu]. Sen, *Kore-eda Hirokazu* 9–29.

———. "Nichijyō no kontei ga yuraide iru sekai ni mukete, chichioya to natta jibun ga egakitai to omou koto" [What I think about becoming a father in a world that is in continual flux]. Sen, *Kore-eda Hirokazu* 235–40.

———. "Serote-pu" [Cellophane tape]. Kore-eda, *Sekai to ima wo kangaeru 1* 371–75.

———. "The Things I Learned from Hou Hsiao-hsien." *Hou Hsiao-hsien*. Trans. Ryan Cook. Ed. Richard Suchenski. Vienna: SYNEMA, 2014. 185.

Kubota Nao and Kore-eda Hirokazu. "Dokyumentari—to fikushion no aida" [Between documentary and fiction]. *Shūkan Shinchō* 33 (Mar. 2014): 166–75.

Kurosawa Kazuko and Kore-eda Hirokazu. "Sugao no Kurosawa Akira wo kataru" [Talking candidly about Kurosawa Akira]. Kore-eda, *Sekai to ima wo kangaeru* 2 267–88.

LaFleur, William R. "Suicide off the Edge of Explicability: Awe in Ozu and Kore'eda." *Film History* 14.2 (2002): 158–65.

Lee, Yong Wook. "The Japanese Challenge to Neoliberalism: Who and What Is 'Normal' in the History of the World Economy?" *Review of International Political Economy* 15.4 (2008): 506–34.

Leitner, Helga, and Eric Sheppard. "'The City Is Dead, Long Live the Net': Harnessing European Interurban Networks for a Neoliberal Agenda." *Spaces of Neoliberalism: Urban Restructuring in North America and Western Europe*. Ed. Neil Brenner and Nik Theodore, 148–71. Oxford: Blackwell, 2002.

Lévi-Strauss, Claude. "The Family." *The View from Afar*. Trans. Joachim Neugroschel and Phoebe Hoss. New York: Basic Books, 1985. 39–62.

Marran, Christine L. "Tracking the Transcendental: Kore'eda Hirokazu's *Maboroshi*." *Film History* 14.2 (2002): 166–69.

Marinov, Robert. "Neoliberal Rationality and the Consumption of Biased News: Theorizing the Neoliberal Subjectivation of News Media Audiences." *Critical Studies in Media Communication* 37.1 (2020): 1–14.

Mathews, Gordon. "Can a 'Real Man' Live for His Family? *Ikigai* and Masculinity in Today's Japan." Roberson and Suzuki, *Men and Masculinities* 109–25.

Matsui, Shigenori. "Fundamental Human Rights and 'Traditional Japanese Values': Constitutional Amendment and Vision of the Japanese Society." *Asian Journal of Comparative Law* 13.1 (July 2018): 59–86.

Michida Yōichi and Kore-eda Hirokazu. "Uchigawa kara no kotoba wo hikidasu to iu sagyō" [The work of pulling words from within]. *Tsukuru* 41.6 (July 2011): 114–19.

Miyamoto Teru. *Maboroshi no hikari*. Tokyo: Shinchōsha, 1983.

Mulvey, Laura. "Visual Pleasure and Narrative Cinema." *Screen* 16.3 (Oct. 1975): 6–18.

Nagata Kazuhiro and Kore-eda Hirokazu. "'Kazoku,' 'jikan,' soshite 'kotoba'" ["Family," "time," and "communication"]. Kore-eda, *Sekai to ima wo kangaeru* 2 61–100.

Nail, Thomas. "What Is an Assemblage?" *SubStance* 46.1 (2017): 21–37.

Noda Makiaki and Kore-eda Hirokazu. "Ikiru imi wo tō mae ni" [Before questioning the meaning of life]. Kore-eda, *Sekai to ima wo kangaeru* 3 167–88.

Nolletti, Arthur. "Introduction: Kore-eda Hirokazu, Director at a Crossroads." *Film Criticism* 35.2/3 (2011): 2–10.

———. "Kore-eda's Children: An Analysis of *Lessons from a Calf*, *Nobody Knows*, and *Still Walking*." *Film Criticism* 35.2/3 (2011): 147–65.

Novick, Peter. *The Holocaust and Collective Memory*. London: Bloomsbury Publishing, 2001.

Ogawa Yōko and Kore-eda Hirokazu. "*Umi yori mo fukaku*: Mō soko ni inai kazoku wo egaku" [*After the Storm*: Depicting a family that is no longer there]. *Kinema Junpō* 1717 (June 2016): 56–63.

Paletz, Gabriel M., and Saito Ayako. "The Halfway House of Memory: An Interview with Hirokazu Kore-eda." *CineAction* Winter 2003: 52–59.

Park, Je Cheol. "Envisioning a Community of Survivors in *Distance* and *Air Doll*." *Film Criticism* 35.2/3 (2011): 166–86.

Pratt, Geraldine, and Rose Marie San Juan. *Film and Urban Space*. Edinburgh: Edinburgh UP, 2014.

Radstone, Susannah. "Cinema and Memory." *Memory: Histories, Theories, Debates*. Ed. Susannah Radstone and Bill Schwarz. New York: Fordham UP, 2010. 325–42.

Rafferty, Terrence. "The Irresistible Drama of Becoming Who You Want to Be." *Atlantic* Apr. 2020. https://www.theatlantic.com/magazine/archive/2020/04/hirokazu-kore-eda-family-drama/606796/.

Rayns, Tony. "Acts That Elicit Sympathy in Viewers." Sen, *Kore-eda Hirokazu* 133–37.

———. "Review: *Still Walking*." *Film Comment* July/Aug. 2009.

Richie, Donald. "Kore-eda's *Maborosi*: Showing Only What Is Necessary." *Film Criticism* 35.2/3 (2011): 37–45.

Rirī Furankī and Kore-eda Hirokazu. "Egakō to omotte iru, sara ni sono saki e" [Showing us while moving into the future]. Kore-eda, *Sekai to ima wo kangaeru 1* 189–222.

———. "Erosu to ikkai taiji shinai to shinenai" [I can't die until I have faced off with sex once]. Sen, *Kore-eda Hirokazu* 30–55.

Risker, Paul. "Questioning the Nature of Family Bonds: An Interview with Hirokazu Kore-eda." *Cineaste* 44.2 (Spring 2019): 42–43.

Roberson, James E. "Japanese Working-Class Masculinities: Marginalized Complexities." Roberson and Suzuki, *Men and Masculinities* 126–43.

Roberson, James E., and Nobue Suzuki. Introduction. Roberson and Suzuki, *Men and Masculinities* 1–19.

Saitō Tamaki and Kore-eda Hirokazu. "Fuikushon no tsuyomi wo ikashite" [Leveraging the power of fiction]. Kore-eda, *Sekai to ima wo kangaeru 3* 135–47.

Schilling, Mark, and Kore-eda Hirokazu. "Kore-eda Hirokazu Interview." *Film Criticism* 35.2/3 (2011): 11–20.

Schofield, Joanna. "Under the Skin: How Filmmakers Affectively Reduce the Space between the Film and the Viewer." *Film Matters* Spring 2014: 44–53.

Schrader, Paul. *Transcendental Style in Film: Ozu, Bresson, Dreyer*. New York: Da Capo Press, 1972.

Shiga Naoya. "Han no hanzai" [Han's crime]. *Shiga Naoya shōsetsu sen* [The selected works of Shiga Naoya]. Tokyo: Iwanami Shoten, 1987. 1:357–75.

Shigesato Itoi and Kore-eda Hirokazu. "Shinsai wo hete, nao erareru mono" [Things gained by experiencing disaster]. Kore-eda, *Sekai to ima wo kangaeru* 2 179–218.

Shildrick, Margrit. "Prosthetic Performativities: Deleuzian Connections and Queer Corporealities." *Deleuze and Queer Theory*. Ed. C. Nigianni and M. Storr. Edinburgh: Edinburgh UP, 2009. 115–33.

———. "Why Should Our Bodies End at the Skin? Embodiment, Boundaries, and Somatechnics." *Hypatia* 30.1 (Winter 2015): 13–29.

Shimamori Michiko and Kore-eda Hirokazu. "Kamera wo hasande, tagai ga seicho shite iku" [Those on both sides of the camera can grow]. Sen, *Kore-eda Hirokazu* 165–93.

Silverman, Kaja. *Male Subjectivity at the Margins*. New York: Routledge, 1992.

Sōda Kazuhiro. "Kore-eda eiga ni okeru dokumentari—no shuhō" [The technique of documentary filmmaking in Kore-eda's films]. Sen, *Kore-eda Hirokazu* 104–09.

Takazaki Toshio and Kore-eda Hirokazu. "Kodomo no nichijyōteki na mesen kara hanarenai koto" [Focusing on the children's everyday gaze]. *Kinema Junpō* 1586 (June 2011): 70–73.

Takeda Satetsu and Kore-eda Hirokazu. "Intabyu" [Interview]. Sen, *Kore-eda Hirokazu* 252–55.

Thanem, Torkild. "The Body without Organs: Nonorganizational Desire in Organizational Life." *Culture and Organization* 10.3 (2004): 203–17.

Thompson, Kristin. "The Concept of Cinematic Excess." *Narrative, Apparatus, Ideology: A Film Theory Reader*. Ed. Philip Rosen. New York: Columbia UP, 1986. 130–42.

Toda Katsura and Kore-eda Hirokazu. "Intabyu" [Interview]. Sen, *Kore-eda Hirokazu* 241–46.

Todoroki Yukio and Kinbara Yuka. "Tettei hihyō taidan, 'Soshite chichi ni naru,' Kore-eda Hirokazu to, Nihon eiga no kazoku no shōzō" [In-depth dialogue: *Like Father, Like Son*, Kore-eda Hirokazu, and a portrait of a Japanese film family]. *Kinema Junpō* 1647 (Oct. 2013): 56–61.

Todoroki Yukio et al. "Rirī Furankī, kazoku no naka no chichi, Osamu, Kore-eda Hirokazu kantoku ga 10 nenkan kangaete kita koto, ikkannsei ga arata na ryōiki e fumidasu" [Rirī Furankī, the father of the family, Osamu, director Kore-eda Hirokazu takes a step into new territory after ten years]. *Kinema Junpō* 1782 (June 2018): 18–22.

Traverso, Enzo. "Presentism: The Politics of Memory in the Age of Neoliberalism." University of California, Berkeley. 14 Sept. 2016. Lecture.

Tsukada Izumi and Andō Sakura. "Andō Sakura—hikareta nowa Kore-eda gumi ni sanka suru to iu koto" [Andō Sakura—to be a part of the Kore-eda Club]. *Kinema Junpō* 1782 (June 2018): 23–25.

Wada-Marciano, Mitsuyo. "Capturing 'Authenticity': Digital Aesthetics in the Post-studio Japanese Cinema." *Canadian Journal of Film Studies* 18.1 (Mar. 2009): 71–93.

———. "A Dialogue through Memories: *Still Walking*." *Film Criticism* 35.2/3 (2011): 110–26.

Yamada, Marc. *Locating Heisei in Japanese Fiction and Film: The Historical Imagination of the Lost Decades*. London: Routledge, 2020.

Yamada Taichi and Kore-eda Hirokazu. "Sasayaka na ichijō, teinei ni eigaku koto" [Elegantly depicting the modesty of every day]. Kore-eda, *Sekai to ima wo kangaeru 1* 259–94.

Yoshimoto Mitsuhiro. *Kurosawa: Film Studies and Japanese Cinema*. Durham, NC: Duke UP, 2000.

Marc Yamada is associate professor of Interdisciplinary Humanities at Brigham Young University. He is the author of *Locating Heisei in Japanese Fiction and Film: The Historical Imagination of The Lost Decades*.

Richard Linklater
David T. Johnson

David Lynch
Justus Nieland

John Sayles
David R. Shumway

Dario Argento
L. Andrew Cooper

Todd Haynes
Rob White

Christian Petzold
Jaimey Fisher

Spike Lee
Todd McGowan

Terence Davies
Michael Koresky

Francis Ford Coppola
Jeff Menne

Emir Kusturica
Giorgio Bertellini

Agnès Varda
Kelley Conway

John Lasseter
Richard Neupert

Paul Thomas Anderson
George Toles

Cristi Puiu
Monica Filimon

Wes Anderson
Donna Kornhaber

Jan Švankmajer
Keith Leslie Johnson

Kelly Reichardt
Katherine Fusco and Nicole Seymour

Michael Bay
Lutz Koepnick

Abbas Kiarostami,
Expanded Second Edition
Mehrnaz Saeed-Vafa and Jonathan Rosenbaum

Lana and Lilly Wachowski
Cáel M. Keegan

Todd Solondz
Julian Murphet

Lucrecia Martel
Gerd Gemünden

Werner Herzog
Joshua Lund

Kore-eda Hirokazu
Marc Yamada

The University of Illinois Press
is a founding member of the
Association of University Presses.

———————————————

University of Illinois Press
1325 South Oak Street
Champaign, IL 61820-6903
www.press.uillinois.edu